DIVAN-E NURBAKHSH

POEMS OF A SUFI MASTER
DR. JAVAD NURBAKHSH

Copyright © 2014 Khaniqahi Nimatullahi Publications

Divan-e Nurbakhsh: Poems of a Sufi Master
By Dr. Javad Nurbakhsh

Khaniqahi Nimatullahi Publications
306 West 11th Street, New York, New York 10014
www.nimatullahi.org

ISBN: 978-0-933546-88-2

All rights are reserved.
No part of this publication may be reproduced, stored in a retrieval system or transmitted in any form or by any means, electronic, mechanical, photocopying, recording or otherwise, without prior permission of KNP, except in the case of brief quotations embodied in critical reviews.

Library of Congress Cataloging-in-Publication Data

Nurbakhsh, Javad.
  [Divan. English]
  Divan-e Nurbakhsh : poems of a Sufi master / Dr. Javad Nurbakhsh.
     pages cm
  Includes bibliographical references and index.
  ISBN 978-0-933546-88-2 (alk. paper)
  1. Sufi poetry, Persian--Translations into English. I. Title.
  PK6561.N79A2 2014
  891'.5513--dc23
                          2014016498

Translated by: Alireza Nurbakhsh, Hossein Kashani,
Jawid Mojaddedi and Robert Sternau
Edited by: Dani Kopoulos and Paul Weber
Designed by: Martin Harris
Production Assistance by: Lolo Saney
Calligraphy by: Seyed Ahmad Shafiei
Printed in the United States of America

CONTENTS

INTRODUCTION	I
NOTE ON THE TRANSLATION	VI
GLOSSARY AND PRONUNCIATION GUIDE	VII
GHAZALS	
The Banquet of the Tavern of Ruin	3
He Is the Truth	9
The Matrix of Thought	10
Why?	12
The Price of Wine	13
The King of *Baqa*	14
Lost	15
Words Accomplish Nothing	16
Our Celebration	17
Come!	18
The King of Love	19
The Dance of Unity	21
The Moment Is Precious	22
The *Khaniqah* of the Dervishes	23
Love's Speech	25
The Pain of Love	26
The Law of Loving-Kindness	27
One Breath	28
The Sanctuary of Sincerity and Purity	29
My Lord	31
Searching for Love	32
The Blind Alley of Life	33
For You	34
Love's Commotion	35
From Him	36
The Dwelling of the Dervish	37
The Commander of Creation	38
All Existence	39
The Fire Temple of Love	40
God and Love	41
The Lantern of Love	42
Yearning for You	43
There Is Naught…	44
Nothing Other Than You	45

The Pavilion of Unity	46
Mysteries of the Heart	47
The Sufi's Retreat	48
The Story of Love	49
The World of Love and Revelry	50
Reputation for Madness	51
Love's Existence	52
The Song of Unity	53
Reassessment of Love	54
Those without Love and Purity	55
One Cannot	56
The Wayward Intellect	57
The Torrent	58
The Human Prey	59
Without Love	60
One Who Knows God	61
The Cane of Heresy	62
The Tavern Door	63
The Distraught Heart	64
The Crazed Heart	65
The Prayer Niche of Supplication	66
Love's Ascension	67
God's House	68
The Divine Reed Player	69
The Treasure Chest of Mysteries	70
Yearning to See You	72
Without You	73
Bewitching Eyes	74
Whoever Becomes Nothing Will Reach God	75
The Candle of Being	76
At the Tavern Door	77
The Season for Anemones	78
The Decree of the Intimates of Mysteries	79
Love Crazed	80
The Basis of Creation	81
The Ocean of Tracelessness	82
Hold On!	83
Don't Acquire!	84
Reproach Is Wrong	85
The Song of Praise	86
The Boastful Are Not Privy to the Path of Loving-Kindness	87
The Creed of the *Rendan*	88

Ask	89
Don't Ask	90
Don't Ask *How* and *Why*	91
The Call of Love	92
The Lord of the Heart	94
The Heart	95
The Tavern's Threshold	96
The Silence of Solitude	97
Mansurian Wine	98
The Followers of Love	99
Arguments	100
Remembering You	102
The Interpreted Sign	103
The Silent Lover	104
Passion for Madness	105
The Fable of Existence	106
The Hope of All Existence	107
The Sign of Tracelessness	108
Transfixed by the Cupbearer's Face	109
Desire for You	110
Longing for You	112
A Lost Heart	113
Alas	114
Transfixed by Idols	115
The Sin of Self-Assertion	116
The World and the Spiritual Realm	117
Discourse on Thoughts	118
Claiming to Love	119
The Reed Pipe and the Player	120
The Miracle of Non-Being	121
I Am Not Me	122
His Splendor	123
Secrets of Love	124
The Epiphany of Your Beauty	125
The Land of "We" and "You"	126
The Passion of Loving	127
Love's Madness	128
The Path of Love	129
Wares of Non-Existence	130
The Seekers of God	131
The Beggars of the Tavern of Ruin	132
Love's Treasure	133

The Work of Loving	134
Craving for Desire	135
The Palace of Loving-Kindness	136
Beauty's Customer	138
Drunk from Intimacy with You	139
The Beggars of Love	140
The Beloved	141
The Waves of the Ocean of Love	142
The Lovers Who Gamble Life Away	143
The Departed Caravan	144
The House of Sincerity and Purity	145
The People of Loving-Kindness	146
Arise!	148
The Threshold of Loving-Kindness	149
The Transitory "I" and "We"	150
The Promise of Seeing Him	151
The Wine-Drenched	152
God-Seeing Eyes	153
Love	154
Wandering Seeker	155
Sing the Song of Unity	156
Behold!	157
The Essence of Contentment	159
"I" and "You"	160
Fidelity from You	161
Surrender	162
Go!	163
He Is the Living, He Is the Truth, He Is *Hu*	164
Go There!	165
The Colorless Wine	167
Don't Go!	168
Tell Me	169
Don't Speak	170
I Say *Haqq, Haqq,* Cry *Hu, Hu*	171
The Talisman of the Self	173
The Name of the Friend	174
What Does It Mean?	176
Severed	177
The New Year	179
La Elaha Ella'Llah	180
From Tavern to Tavern	182
Traveler on the Path	183

The Broken-Winged Bird	184
District to District	185
He Is the One, the Eternal, without Likeness and Alive	186
The Soul of Existence	187
The Endearing and Loving Companion	188
There Is Nothing but God	189
You Were There	190
Love and Life	191
O Pious Ascetic	192
The Love-Teaching Glance	193
Love's Bazaar	194
The Circle of Unity	195
The Mysteries of Creation	197
What Do You Know?	198
The Tavern's Prosperity	199
To Whom Are You Praying?	200
The Source of Joy	201
Love Is Sweet	202
Misconception	203
Whether You Like It or Not	204
The Display of Creation	205
The Drop and the Ocean	206
The Crazy Intellect	207
He Is, There Is Nothing but He	208
My New Year Is You	210
The Master's Grace	212
Hu, Haqq	214
Sama	216

MASNAVIS

The Tavern of Ruin	223
Reason and Love	225
The Sufis' *Sama*	227
Opening to *Sama*	228
He	229
The Dog	230
Sea Wave	231
The Illusion of "I" and "You"	233
The Image of Existence	234
Listen to God	235
Love and the Heart	239
Listen to the Wine	250
Listen to the Reed Player	253

Listen to the Master	257
The Silence and *Adab* of the Sufis	262
Love and Desire	266
The Honeybee and the Blossom	274
The Remembrance of God	278
Listen to the Cupbearer	284
The Prayer of *Sama*	290

ODES TO THE CUPBEARER
Ode to the Cupbearer 1	295
Ode to the Cupbearer 2	296
Ode to the Cupbearer 3	298

RESPONSE POEMS
Response to a Wayfarer	305
In Answer to a Letter from a Traveler on the Path	307

PERSIAN NEW VERSE (*SHE'R-E NOW*)
Remembering You	313
You Are My Poem!	314
Be Silent!	315
Ocean	316

45 QUATRAINS — 319

TRUTHS OF LOVE — 329

NOTES — 387

INTRODUCTION

Listening to my father's poetry was part of my upbringing. His poems were sung in weekly Sufi gatherings in the Tehran *khaniqah*, where I grew up, along with the poetry of Rumi, 'Attar, 'Eraqi, Shah Nimatullah and other Sufi poets. Sufi poetry is meant to be sung out loud in Sufi gatherings in order to instill in listeners a sense of longing for love and the truth.

My father composed the bulk of his poetry in his twenties while he was a medical student at the University of Tehran, and later on while he worked as a young doctor in Bam, Iran. The first edition of his *Divan* was published in 1956 when he was thirty years old, although some of his poems were published earlier in a small pamphlet in 1953. He continued to write poetry well into his seventies.

He was blessed with a poetic bent from an early age and he composed his first *masnavi* at the age of sixteen. In this poem, entitled "The Dog," he rates a dog's fidelity higher than that of human beings. Most of his poetry is in the ghazal form so prevalent among Persian Sufi poets. His *Divan* in fact contains more than 180 ghazals, compared with forty-five quatrains, twenty *masnavis* and fifty-five five-verse poems known collectively as *Haqayeq al-mahabba fi daqayeq al-wahda* (Truths of love in moments of unity).

My father was not in the habit of dating his poems; thus we do not have an accurate chronological order of all of them. However, his poetry was published more than thirteen times in the original Persian in Iran, and it is possible to trace the chronological order of some of the poems through the date of the edition in which they first appear.

My father's poetry as a whole deals with the central themes of Sufism: that the ego is the obstacle that separates human beings from the experience of the truth; that love, in contrast to the intellect or reason, is the means by which the Sufi may be freed from the bonds of the ego; and that God, or the Truth, is the only being, and all created beings simply reflect this single reality.

To a greater degree than virtually all other Sufi poetry, my father's poetic treatment of these central themes serves to instruct the reader about the Sufi path and the nature of reality more than it seeks to give poetic expression to his inner states. This is especially apparent in a series of long poems in the *masnavi* style that my father wrote in his sixties. In these poems he articulates in clear and direct language answers to such questions as: What are the qualities of a true master? What is the remembrance of God? What is needed to be a lover of God? How can one attain union with God? It's as if in these later poems he was using the more flexible form of the *masnavi* to summarize teachings that appear within the more formal structures and traditional imagery of his early ghazals.

Central among these teachings is the exposition of the ego as being the biggest stumbling block on the Sufi path. In one ghazal after another he stresses the need to be liberated from the ego (or, as he refers to it throughout his *Divan*, "I" and "you" or "I" and "we").

Self-assertion is a sin
that the Friend does not forgive;

with a single glance,
He cut me off from "I" and "we."

How may one be freed from the ego? In keeping with centuries of Sufi teaching, my father's poetry stresses that love (*'eshq*) alone makes it possible for a person to overcome his or her ego in the journey towards God.

Love is to flee from "I" and "we" and
to rest in the shade of the Friend.

It is to remove oneself from the center and
to pull Him instead to the core of one's soul.

In contrast to much of Sufi poetry, which tends to disparage the intellect (*'aql*) because it cannot free one from the ego, my father's poetry views the intellect as a double-edged sword requiring constant vigilance. To the extent that it helps people and eases some of life's difficulties it is indeed a servant of the heart.

Compared to conventional reason we are mad,
yet, in this world we are wiser than any sage.

The problem arises when the intellect becomes the servant of the ego; it is then that its greatest achievements and discoveries become catastrophes for humanity.

In the eyes of the Master of Love,
the intellect is but a child,
who, from lack of discernment,
has become absorbed in illusion.

The theme of the unity of being (*wahdat al-wujud*), is another of the central tenets of Sufism that is expressed throughout my father's *Divan*, often using the traditional metaphors common to many Sufi poets.

From the heart of every atom
I hear, "the Friend, the Friend."
So don't even see the atom,
for there is really nothing but Him.

The ocean's outward manifestations
    are called bubble and wave,
yet in reality it is all water,
    whether droplet, stream or sea.

I would be remiss if I did not point out that for my father Sufism is all about practice and experience, and what is known as theoretical Sufism is meaningful only if accompanied by personal experience. Thus, in his *Divan* the exposition of Sufi themes is often presented in the language of intense personal experience.

Moreover, alongside his many poems that are intended to guide seekers my father also wrote very personal poems that give voice to his inner states and feelings. Among these are a few poems he wrote in *she'r-e now* (so-called Persian new verse), in which all formal structure and rhyming formats are abandoned. He is perhaps the only Sufi master to have experimented with this style, which allows for the expression of heartfelt states without the limitations inherent in the classical forms.

You asked of me free verse:
    You wanted...
A poem emerging from my heart
    without deliberation,
A fervor rising from my breast
    unembellished,
For all to see its nakedness
Devoid of everything that I am and have ever been,
    free of everything I know and have ever known,
        beyond the old and the new world.
So what is my free verse?
    Listen.........it is You!

Viewed as a whole, the *Divan-e Nurbakhsh* contains a wide variety of Sufi poetry that gives expression to the complex and subtle meanings of various concepts about the nature of truth, love, mystical states and the spiritual path. But I should point out that my father communicated in a simple, but subtle, manner, and his poems are perhaps best approached from a similar attitude. As he has written,

If you have heard that we are rendan
    it is true;
but if you are simple,
    we will be simple with you.

Perhaps the most fitting conclusion of this foreword is to cite a few lines of his poem, "One Breath," which is written for the benefit of all human beings:

If you spend this moment laughing,
    the world will reflect your joy.
But if you fall into depression,
    the whole world will be in mourning.

Don't give your heart to this
    transitory world
with all its ups and downs,
    its twists and turns.

Bring joy to another's heart;
    and be joyful yourself
for the highest gain in the world
    is this.

Take care, Nurbakhsh,
    not to hurt any heart;
accomplishing this is more dear
    than any crown or throne.

Alireza Nurbakhsh
London, March 2014

NOTE ON THE TRANSLATION

This translation is based on the Persian original of *Divan-e Nurbakhsh* (Tehran, 1379/2000). The poems therefore follow the order of presentation in that work, which, for the ghazals, is based alphabetically on the rhyme, as is the convention in Persian. It should be noted that the original Persian *Divan* on which this translation is based includes, in addition to the ghazals, Dr. Nurbakhsh's quatrains (*roba'iyyat*), his poems in the *masnavi* form, his new verse poems (*she'r-e now*), his odes to the cupbearer (*saqinameha*), and also his collection of five-verse poems entitled "Truths of Love" (*Haqayeq al-mahabba fi daqayeq al-wahda*). This new translation therefore presents poems by Dr. Nurbakhsh in all major poetic forms in a single volume, and includes new translations directly from the Persian of poems that have been published previously in two different books and various journals, as well as poems that have never been translated before.

As far as possible, the English equivalents of technical terms have been provided, rather than giving the original in transliteration and relying on explanatory notes. Where it is provided, the transliteration of names and terms has been simplified to such a degree that no diacritics are used. It is designed simply to help the reader use correct Persian pronunciation when reading the poems. Definitions of terms, identification of names, and guidelines for pronunciation are provided in the Glossary, which is situated at the front of this book. This serves as an indispensable aid to understanding the translations. Endnotes are also provided to give clarifications of certain terms and offer alternative translations for those verses that intentionally have more than one meaning.

Capitalization has been used sparingly, and only when reference is made to God. This includes, in addition to the pronouns and titles commonly used in English, the ninety-nine names of God of the Sufi tradition, as well as certain poetic and philosophical terms.

Instead of a more poetical rendering, the translators have striven to provide as literal a rendition as possible in fluent and accessible modern English. This has enabled the retention of specific terms of Sufi symbolism which have a significant place in Dr. Nurbakhsh's poetry (see his own *Sufi Symbolism* series published by Khaniqahi Nimatullahi Publications). The translators acknowledge that other readings of some verses are possible and that some terms may have multiple definitions; the translators' choice has been based on the criterion of contextual coherence. As noted above, where multiple meanings are deliberately intended, these have been mentioned in the endnotes.

GLOSSARY AND PRONUNCIATION GUIDE

adab (pronounced aadaab)
In most contexts, courtesy, code of conduct, proper conduct, proper manners, decorum, or proper etiquette. For Sufi mystics, the following definition applies: "…the etiquette of gnosis occurs when the gnostic is with God wherever he is and at whatever time, and is in conformity with God's will."

> *Etiquette lies not in worshipping properly*
> *or striving for one's entitlement;*
> *Make yourself dust — make yourself nothing:*
> *that is what etiquette means!*
>
> J. Nurbakhsh, *Sufi Symbolism*, Vol. XI, pp.1–3

Ayaz (pronounced Ayaaz)
See Mahmud and Ayaz below.

baqa (pronounced *baqaa*)
Subsistence in God, permanence in God. "In Sufi terminology, subsistence signifies the experience of oneself abiding in God after one has become annihilated from oneself.…" (J. Nurbakhsh, *Sufi Symbolism*, Vol. XII, pp. 137–139)

Bayazid (pronounced Baayazid)
Bayazid Bestami (d. 874), an eminent Sufi from what is now North Central Iran. He is a highly popular figure in Persian Sufi literature, in particular because of the many bold and controversial statements he is reported to have made, such as, "There is nothing under my cloak but God."

Covenant
Also known as the Pre-eternal Covenant of *Alast*, or simply *Alast*. It is a reference to the Qur'anic verse 7:172, "Am I not your Lord (*alasto be rabbekom*)?" This is the question posed by God to mankind when mankind was pure spirit in the presence of God, before entering the world. In response to this question, mankind testified that God is their Lord by saying "Yes!"

fana (pronounced *fanaa*)
Annihilation of the self in God. "The reality of annihilation is being obliterated in God's attributes, where all one's own attributes, including one's very consciousness of this annihilation and awareness of being annihilated, are obliterated in the attributes of God." (J. Nurbakhsh, *Sufi Symbolism*, Vol. XII, pp. 129–134)

faqr
Spiritual poverty, "an individual's spiritual impoverishment and need for God." (J. Nurbakhsh, *Spiritual Poverty in Sufism*, p. 4)

Farhad (pronounced Farhaad)
See Farhad and Shirin below.

Farhad and Shirin
Two lovers in the Persian poet Nezami Ganjavi's (1149–1209) epic love story "Khosrow and Shirin." Khosrow II, the Sassanian king, is in love with Shirin, an Armenian princess. Farhad, an architect, also falls in love with Shirin. Khosrow, wishing to get rid of his rival, exiles Farhad to the Bistun Mountains and assigns him the task of carving stairs out of the hard cliff rock, promising him that upon completing the work he will be allowed to marry Shirin. Instead, Khosrow misleads Farhad into believing Shirin has died, and in his grief Farhad jumps from a cliff to his death.

Hallaj (pronounced Hallaaj)
Mansur al-Hallaj (855–922), a Sufi mystic who was accused of heretical doctrines and for his ecstatic utterances, such as "I am the Truth" (*ana 'l-Haqq*). After many court hearings he was convicted and publicly executed in Baghdad.

Haqq
A name of God, meaning Truth or Reality, it is used frequently by Sufis in chanting remembrance of God (see *zekr* below).

Hayy
A name of God, meaning the Ever-Living, it is used frequently by Sufis in chanting remembrance of God (see *zekr* below).

Hu
The name for God's Essence, it also means simply "He," and is used frequently by Sufis in chanting remembrance of God (see *zekr* below).

"I" and "we" / "we" and "I"
A state of being characterized by self-assertion, self-centeredness, self-display, self-aggrandizement, setting one's self apart, giving oneself priority over others.

"I" and "you"
A state of being characterized by the view: "I am apart from you, you are different from me, my interests do not coincide with yours, we are not united."

khaniqah (pronounced *khaaneqaah*)
The center of congregational worship for Sufis.

Khezr
A figure usually identified with Enoch/Elias, and described in the Qur'an (18:65) as someone who has been taught knowledge from God's presence. He is the archetypal spiritual guide in the Sufi tradition. The Qur'anic story about Khezr (18:65–82) describes Moses as seeking to become his disciple in order to learn some of Khezr's special knowledge. Moses is warned that he does not have the patience required, but is finally accepted on the condition that he should not question Khezr about anything. Moses fails to refrain from questioning Khezr, and, on the third such occasion, Khezr dismisses him.

La elaha ella'Llah **(pronounced *laa elaaha ella'llaah*)**
The first part of the Islamic declaration of faith, meaning "there is no god but God," which testifies to divine unity. It is often understood by Sufis to mean that nothing exists but God. This formula is commonly used in chanting remembrance of God (see *zekr* below).

Layli
See Layli and Majnun below.

Layli and Majnun
Layli (also known as Layla) and Majnun (lit. madman), are the archetypal pair of lovers in the Arabo-Persian Sufi literary tradition. Majnun is prevented from marrying Layli by her father, and wanders naked in the desert as if possessed, thereby earning his name. Layli eventually dies of grief and Majnun rushes to her grave where he also dies and is buried beside her. These legendary lovers came from the north Arabian tribe of Amir. In 1188, the Persian poet Nezami forged this love story into a great epic poem of more than 4000 stanzas, giving this simple nomadic lore a mystical dimension.

Mahmud
See Mahmud and Ayaz below.

Mahmud and Ayaz (pronounced Ayaaz)
The protagonists in a famous myth in Persian Sufi literature, in which Malek Ayaz, the favorite slave of Shah Mahmud of Ghazna (r. 997–1030), wins his master's love through his unconditional and selfless devotion to him and is rewarded with the throne of Lahore in 1021.

Majnun
See Layli and Majnun above.

qalandar **(pl. *qalandaran*; pronounced *qalandaraan*)**
Wandering dervish. "The *qalandar* (a detached dervish of a rapturous state) is liberated from all bonds and has no interest in clothing, food or spiritual practices. He is detached totally from rejection or acceptance by others." (J. Nurbakhsh, *Sufi Symbolism*, Vol. VI, p. 123)

rend **(pl. *rendan*; pronounced *rendaan*)**
"…in Sufi terminology, the rend is one who is liberated from the bonds of etiquette and the conventions of society and who is delivered from the world and its inhabitants. Outwardly he is a person of blame, while inwardly he is blameless." (J. Nurbakhsh, *Sufi Symbolism,* Vol. VI, pp. 119–121)

sama **(pronounced *samaa*)**
"Though usually translated as 'spiritual music,' *sama* literally means 'hearing.' In the terminology of Sufism, it is listening with the ear of the heart to music in the most profound sense — poetry, melodies, tunes, and rhythmic harmonies — while being in a special state so deeply plunged in love that there is no taint of self left within awareness. In this sense, *sama* is called the 'call of God.'" (J. Nurbakhsh, *The Path*, p.75)

Shirin
See Farhad and Shirin above.

"we" and "I"
See "I" and "we" above.

"we" and "you"
A state of being characterized by the view: "we are apart from you, you people are not like us, we are mostly superior to you."

Yazid
Yazid ebn Mo'awiya ebn Abi Sufyan (647– 683) was the second ruler of the Umayyad caliphate. This was the first inherited caliphate, which angered many prominent Muslims. Hosayn, the Prophet's grandson, challenged Yazid; he and 75 of his followers and family members were eventually massacred on Yazid's orders at the battle of Kerbala (October 10th 680), where they were vastly outnumbered by Yazid's army.

zekr
Literally, remembrance. For Sufi mystics, it means the remembrance of God by means of the repetition of His names (e.g., *Haqq*, *Hu*) or short religious formulae about Him (e.g., *La elaha ella'Llah*). This repetition, which is the heart of Sufi practice in all its diverse schools, can be performed silently, under one's breath, or loudly in an assembly. Sufis are instructed to give total and uncompromising attention to God during *zekr*. The *zekr* is transmitted to the disciple in a special manner by the Sufi master or sheikh. "Through the inculcation of *zekr*, the master instructs the disciple how to be in continuous remembrance of the Divine… When the disciple becomes continually involved in the remembrance of God, his being gradually becomes liberated from egotistical and selfish qualities and illuminated by the Divine Attributes and Divine Nature…" (J. Nurbakhsh, *In the Paradise of the Sufis*, pp.19–20)

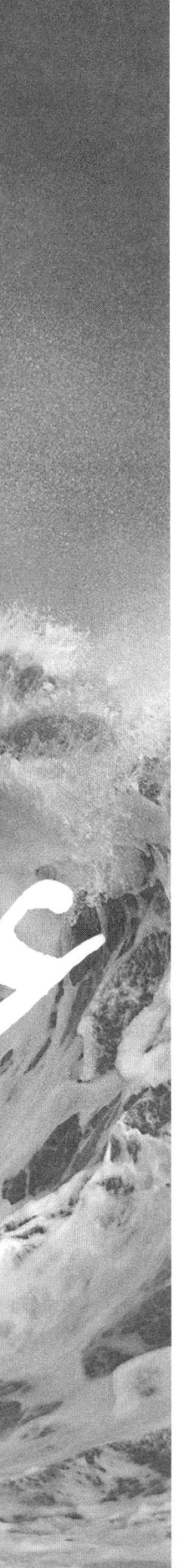

Ghazals

THE BANQUET OF THE TAVERN OF RUIN

I praise the tavern of ruin
    and the people of vision there;
they have no thought of this world
    or the next
        there.

In the alley of *fana* neither
    verdant nor withered appears;
nothing is fruitful
    or fruitless
        there.

Self display won't find its way
    to this festival of fidelity;
discussion of this world and the next
    is very brief
        there.

In the world of "we" and "you"[1]
    there is reason to fear danger;
when "we" and "you" is dispelled
    there will be no danger
        there.

The good and evil in this world come
    from the good and bad inside you;
when you become all good,
    there will be no "good" or "evil"
        there.

When you find fault with this world
    the fault is really your own;
nothing but beauty
    and serenity prevails
        there.

When you reject others
    you are the rejected one.
How could rejection or acceptance
    ever be found
        there?

This knowledge of yours is but a toy
    of the imagination, not a virtue;
the knowledge of every expert
    will be useless
        there.

The humility, selflessness
    and abjection of the *rend*
is considered the crown and belt
    of power
        there.

In the book of Unity you find nothing
    but the lesson of Truth;
pedantic learning is worthless
        there.

Unless you erase the image of self
    from heart and soul
don't even think about
    traveling
        there.

There is nothing but the Light of God,
    the Eye of God and the Face of God;
what is "other than God" is not found
        there.

Man and creation,
    in bewilderment and remorse,
have cast down
    their shields
        there.

The falcon of the intellect
    is too weak to fly there;
nothing but the bird of loving-kindness
    spreads its wings
        there.

No name, no trace,
    no custom, no way;
neither guide nor traveler
    is known
        there.

The life span of the world,
    from pre- to post-eternity,
from beginning to end,
    is not even a moment
        there.

Surrendering one's head, risking one's life,
    and breaking the self
are known as greatness,
    conquest and victory
        there.

In that tavern, the wanderers of God
    find the comfort they seek;
the vagrants of God
    won't be homeless
        there.

This imaginary existence, which is
    the source of our shame,
is even more unreal
    than fantasy and speculation
        there.

Selflessness is the source
    of all kinship;
poverty is considered
    prosperity and abundance
        there.

On that meadow only the flower
	of Unity grows;
but for the palm tree of loving-kindness
	nothing bears fruit
		there.

Although the haunters of that tavern
	cannot tell head from foot,
not every foolish vagabond
	can enter
		there.

Unless you give up
	self-existence
you will be neither
	destitute nor esteemed
		there.

In the state of oblivion
	there is no asking for a cure.
Since there is no sting
	how can there be need for a lancet
		there?

Your self-existence
	is the price of admission;
nothing is sold
	for gold or silver
		there.

One in pain and in need of a cure
	cannot be found there;
there is no yearning or
	flirtation
		there.

This place is beyond whatever
	you can conceive of;
the arrow of imagination
	cannot reach
		there.

These manifest patterns
    are figments of your thought;
when you no longer exist
    these forms won't be
        there.

There is but one Being,
    and He is oblivious to supplication;
wailing and sighing till dawn
    won't open a way
        there.

The tavern's sacred grounds are free
    from all piety and self-display;
many centuries of devotion
    have been rendered useless
        there.

No lover, no beloved
    to need any wine;
no reed pipe, no player
    to need sugar cane
        there.

Where are words and speech
    that may roar like a tempest?
Where are moist eyes
    to spill jewel-like tears
        there?

All agitation and tumult come from
    rawness and imperfection;
When there is no imperfection,
    no passion or uproar will exist
        there.

There is no name or trace
    of your fame there;
no one but the Beloved
    is celebrated
        there.

Without speaker, without listener,
    without Moses, without Sinai,
the cry of "I am the Truth"[2]
    comes from every bush
        there.

Unless you abandon arguments,
    you will never find your way there,
for light is not bestowed
    upon every sightless one
        there.

Our hope lies in this:
    that one day,
by the grace of love,
    we may lay down our heads
        there.

HE IS THE TRUTH

O minstrel, strum your lute
    and pluck the high notes tonight.
O singer, open your song
    with, "He is the Truth."

The heart's dilemma can't be solved
    by following many gods;
entrust your affairs
    to the One Unique Lord.

Leave the book about the world and its people
    for the sane and sober;
inscribe the pages of your book
    with the madness of love.

Abandon this bodily form
    and read the tablet of the heart
so that God's love
    may lift the veil from your soul's eye.

I remain your lover, O God,
    surrendered and content,
whether You counsel me
    or chastise me.

You are for me the manifest Truth.
    You are the hidden and the revealed.
I behold Your presence
    everywhere, in every moment.

Not only has Nurbakhsh's heart and soul
    become illumined by You,
but the entire creation exists
    through the grace of Your light.

THE MATRIX OF THOUGHT

From the matrix of thought
    we have washed away the desire for You,
never to imagine
    communion with You.

You and I united!
    It is an impossible hope, I know.
By one's own feet, no one can traverse
    the path to You.

You, the lover of Your own face,
    are the Beloved.
How then, can anyone but You
    drink up Your jug of wine?

The heart that truly loves You
    is none other than You;
in temperament and nature,
    Your lovers resemble You.

In the creed of love, Your hair
    is the veil covering Your face;
that veil can't be brushed aside
    with the hand of self.

Our tongues do not describe You
    as You really are;
better they were cut off
    than disgrace Your name.

Not freed from the vanity
    of outward color and scent,
we are drunk from "I" and "you."[1]
    How then can we still crave Your fragrance?

Entangled in the bonds of creation and space,
    imprisoned in dimensions,
it is only out of heedlessness
    that we keep searching for You.

Nurbakhsh, do not think
    about the fountain of the sun,
for a wave from the ocean of *fana*
    has washed you away.

WHY?

O Ravisher of hearts! You accept me,
    but why do You want me disgraced?
You pull my heart with Your braids,
    but why in every direction?

Each moment, in a different way, You defeat
    contenders at love's backgammon;
I have lost my self from the very first,
    why do You seek to defeat me yet again?

In love's marketplace
    I closed my eyes to all existence;
since this is a clear gain,
    what more should I want?

You want the mansion of the heart
    emptied of strangers and for Yourself alone.
Why then have You become
    a companion to all?

Having told us that only the believer's heart
    is Your throne,
why, then, do You display Your beauty unconcerned
    upon every wall, through every door?

And if, O Nurbakhsh, the stranger's ears
    can't hear the speech of the soul,
why, then, do you create
    such a commotion?

THE PRICE OF WINE

For a lifetime the fire of love
    burned my heart and soul,
until the Beloved taught me
    the lover's way.

Jealous love gave me no chance
    to cry out;
to keep me silent
    the Beloved sewed my lips tight.

Like a moth I circled around Him
    ecstatically for so long
that He burned me like a candle
    and set me alight in every gathering.

For ages He preserved me
    in the heart of time
so I should now proclaim aloud the
    whisperings of love.

I am the servant of the master of the Magi,[1]
    for he bought me from myself
and sold me in the tavern
    for the price of wine.

Inspired by the Beloved's breath,
    Nurbakhsh said drunkenly,
"For a lifetime the fire of love
    burned my heart and soul."

THE KING OF *BAQA*

My eyes don't rest
    on any face but Yours.
I go towards no place
    other than Your district.

I am a dry, withered tree;
    burning is my art.
Except for this, I bear no fruit
    in the garden of love.

O Cupbearer, pour what wine You will;
    I am surrendered like an empty cup.
In my heart there is no complaint;
    I have no tearful eyes.

In Your sanctuary, I am safe
    and content with Your bliss.
What worry if I am
    leafless and barren?

When I entered the tavern of ruin, I saw
    that before the majesty
of Your presence
    there was no trace of me.

I had always desired
    to know You;
since I have known You
    I know nothing else.

I bestow light because I have always
    wanted only You;
I have had no desire or concern
    for other than You.

LOST

Beloved of my soul,
    You seek me out in every land
to disgrace me
    before people.

Whomever I look at,
    You are the one in my sight —
do you wish to make me
    love-crazed for You?

I am the lover
    seated at Your door,
but not concerned whether or not
    You open it for me.

When You became the customer,
    I sold myself to You;
now it is Your choice
    how to deal with me.

You want me totally,
    always and everywhere,
but only to deny me
    in everyone's eyes.

I died in your district
    in remembrance of Your face —
may You revive me
    with a breath!

O Light Bestower of the soul,
    O soother of the heart,
I am lost —
    how can You ever find me?

WORDS ACCOMPLISH NOTHING

Each time that people
    disturb our state,
our reaction is to give in
    to words.

Through dialogue and discourse
    people gain credence and respect;
as for us, words became
    the sign of our imperfection.

In the valley of love all discourse
    becomes nonsense;
hence, there is no benefit gained
    from our chattering.

Whatever the rationalists
    have said and written
has been just the discourse of the ego,
    meant to keep us occupied.

Words accomplish nothing
    in the banquet of love;
let our time then
    pass in silence.

We don't deny what people may imagine,
    but they will never even catch up
with the dust cloud stirred up by the flight
    of our imagination.

Nurbakhsh, the blade of the tongue
    severs the link
that connects your inner mind
    with Us.

OUR CELEBRATION

O Inspirer of hearts and vision,
    O You in Whose hands rest
the being and non-being
    of all manifest things,

O Bestower of vitality
    to all created existence,
O Bestower of spirit
    to the being of the newly-born,

It is not for us to ask You
    for what we lack,
O You, the ultimate goal
    of the fugitives from self.

You have given to all
    whatever they need.
You are too sublime for words,
    and far beyond what ears have heard.

In pre-eternity
    Your bounty inscribed
upon the tablet of the unseen
    whatever was right for each one.

Today is our festival —
    O You, the object of celebration
for the renouncers of all familiar comforts,
    visit us today!

Since You became the object
    of celebration for Nurbakhsh,
he no longer takes notice
    of created beings.

COME!

We have fallen to our knees
    in Your district — come to us!
We have abandoned the valley
    of the ego — come!

For a lifetime we have been devotees
    in Your sanctuary;
O companion of those liberated
    from self — come!

On the path to union with You
    we have relinquished all;
O existence of all that is — come!

We have thrown away our existence
    on the path of Your love;
You who are without concern
    and difficult to befriend — come!

Through yearning for You, we are unconscious
    of ourselves.
Of this You are aware, for You created
    this unrest — come!

Desiring to see You,
    we left our selves.
It is now time
    to uncover Your face — come!

Nurbakhsh lost himself
    to find You.
Enough of Your disdain,
    with kindness come to us.

THE KING OF LOVE

Lightning flashed from above the throne
    of the realm of possibilities,
and from its radiance was born
    the form of created things.

With coquettish glances and amorous jests,
    He gave the command "Be!"[1]
and brought forth
    so much beauty and grace.

From pre- to post-eternity
    is less than a moment;
know that the premises and the implications
    of all arguments make but one point.

From your point of view alone
    destiny is fulfilled in time.
Created beings travel through stages
    that are only in your mind.

Like children who build toy houses
    with blocks of wood,
you construct a created world with your
    observations.

Don't confuse the toy
    with the real thing;
don't be infatuated
    with flattery and praise.

In the eyes of the master of love
    the intellect is but a child
who, from lack of discernment,
    has become absorbed in illusion.

Burn the pages
      and wash clean the notebooks;
all that has been compiled
      still falls short of the dignity of love.

O Nurbakhsh,
      whatever the intellectuals may write
is but the myth of idols
      and their temples.

It takes a king[2] of love
      to behead the idols
with the sword of his jealousy,
      and to cast them down.

THE DANCE OF UNITY

Come, for the hand of fate
    has shot an arrow and hit the mark;
it has placed the legend of Your beautiful face
    upon every tongue.

What manner of riot was it
    that called forth Your splendor? I do not know,
but it snatched the mystic from himself
    and rendered the Sufi homeless.

Your flirtatious glance
    has been a legend for ages;
it has caused an uproar
    even among those familiar with You.

Through attraction, the firmament reflected
    the agitation of the heart
in the dance of Unity and fervor
    that it displayed.

How wondrous,
    that at the marketplace of yearning
the expounder of love spoke of Your qualities,
    leaving the people gathered there speechless!

I praise the skill of love's hand:
    with a single arrow from the bowstring
it stitched together
    a hundred thousand hearts.

The source of the sun still
    bestows light
from the radiance
    that Your beauty cast upon the world.

THE MOMENT IS PRECIOUS

Pour us an overflowing goblet, O cupbearer,
    the moment is precious.
In the grip of time and space,
    the moment is precious.

The revolving of the heavens
    gave no one a chance.
Release the toil and burden of the world;
    the moment is precious.

Fill the cup with wine —
    the lover is not concerned
with the workings of time;
    the moment is precious.

In the audience hall of love,
    reason is silent.
Leave all words and speech behind;
    the moment is precious.

This day is for revelry, drunkenness
    and loving.
Forget tomorrow and look not for its signs;
    the moment is precious.

The *rendan* in our banquet
    have no care for tomorrow,
knowing that both inwardly and outwardly,
    the moment is precious.

Each moment spent with wine
    and the Beloved —
listen to Nurbakhsh,
    that moment is precious.

THE *KHANIQAH* OF THE DERVISHES

Come, the haven of the devout
    is here.
Come, the Kaaba of pure lovers
    is here.

Come to the tavern
    of the heart-possessing mystics.
God is the cupbearer at this banquet;
    the Almighty is here.

Don't go to the monastery —
    paradise is all they grant;
come to the quarters of the tavern-dwellers,
    for God is here.

Don't say that faithfulness and purity have vanished,
    that compassion is lost.
Come, for purity is the code
    and fidelity the custom here.

If you are fickle in your desires,
    relinquish the desire for us;
but if you pine for God,
    come, the remedy is here.

Do not wander about the world,
    O love-sick one.
Come, the doctor of love bears witness
    that the remedy is here.

Step into this sacred realm
    with respect,
for the prayer niche and the sanctuary
    of the purified are here.

If you wish to reach the shore of love
    with ease, come!
For the ship, the captain,
    and the ocean are all here.

Error cannot enter the precincts
    of the people of God;
if you imagine otherwise,
    that is the error here.

Don't look down on
    the *khaniqah* of the dervishes,
since Gabriel is in attendance
    as a servant here.

New life is bestowed
    upon seekers of the path of love;
let the destitute on the Beloved's path know
    their provision is here.

This is the assembly of intimacy
    for those enamored with God;
the soul is enraptured
    and the heart expanded here.

Love is beyond
    what can be expressed, it is true.
But hush! The primary school
    of God's friends is here.

The dust of its threshold
    can grant a whole world's wishes,
for the sincere dervishes
    leave tracks here.

Here, don't speak
    of "friend" and "stranger";
know that every stranger
    is a friend here.

The light-bestowing nature
    of this *khaniqah* is envied by all,
for the place of martyrdom[1] of Reza,[2]
    the King of Faith, is here.

LOVE'S SPEECH

Love's speech
    is beyond words and meanings.
For love, there is another speaker,
    another language.

The pretender challenged, saying,
    "Speak of love."
But words are wasted on one
    whose heart is deaf.

He who knows the lover's world
    hears only
the whisperings of love
    and kindness.

Love speaks a tongue
    unknown to ordinary people;
leave behind their babble
    with its headaches.

One who denies love will never grasp
    our words;
nothing we could say would ever move
    his lifeless heart.

In the creed of loving-kindness
    there is no aimless talk;
only the bankrupt chatter
    behind every door.

Nurbakhsh, from love's breath
    your speech is eloquent,
embraced by the heart
    of every clear-sighted mystic.

THE PAIN OF LOVE

For one who sees truly,
    love's pain is itself the remedy.
But this mystery is revealed
    only to those afflicted with it.

That lover who has left the realm of the self
    is a stranger to all.
How then could he ever
    be cunning?

Love is an attraction that drags multiplicity
    away from the heart;
the spirit of Unity that it bestows
    is free from all desires.

Love is a ladder
    on the path toward God,
a ladder to that place where
    "God is wherever you look."[1]

Only "I am God"[2] is ever uttered
    at the stage of love;
this secret is known
    to none other than God.

Do not conceive of love
    as a pain without cure;
love is a snare set by God —
    a sanctuary, not a calamity.

O Nurbakhsh, since the lover
    has no awareness of self,
to say he is cunning
    would be a grave mistake.

THE LAW OF LOVING-KINDNESS

By the law of loving-kindness,
    this I have decreed:
any mystic's claim that is based on intellect
    is void.

Perfection captivates
    and absorbs imperfection;
he who is not offended by imperfection
    is, in truth, perfected.

The seeker of shores
    will never drown in the ocean of love;
one who seeks dry land
    is not a lover.

Although on the way of the lover
    there is none but the Beloved,
rapture and attraction, effacement,[1] extinction[2]
    and sobriety[3] are also states to be experienced.

The eye of discrimination is blinded
    by the light of union;
he who imagines himself united with the Beloved
    has no discernment.

The wine drinkers are drunk and enraptured
    with the cupbearer at their side.
Here, anyone who remains sober
    is guilty of negligence.

O Nurbakhsh, we spent our days
    in the worship of wine
since we learned that life without wine
    is lived in vain.

ONE BREATH

From pre- to post-eternity
    is but a single breath,
a breath free of all these
    high and low melodies.

Treasure this breath,
    this moment you now enjoy.
Spend it in happiness; there is
    no time for sorrow.

Once this moment has passed,
    it is gone forever.
Your remaining time is less
    than the very least you can imagine.

If you spend this moment laughing,
    the world will reflect your joy.
But if you fall into depression,
    the whole world will seem to be in mourning.

Don't give your heart to this
    transitory world
with all its ups and downs,
    its twists and turns.

Bring joy to another's heart;
    and be joyful yourself,
for the highest gain in the world
    is this.

Take care, Nurbakhsh,
    not to hurt any heart;
accomplishing this is more dear
    than any crown or throne.

THE SANCTUARY OF SINCERITY AND PURITY

The sanctuary of sincerity and purity
    is the retreat of the dervishes.
The breath of the Holy Spirit
    is the speech of the dervishes.

O you who are caught up in the world
    and seek to raise your status there,
lofty placelessness is the lowest level reached
    by the dervishes.

How long will you seek
    the cause of creation?
The purpose of creating humankind
    is to produce dervishes.

Being obliterated by the arrow of fate,
    affirming contentment with the will of God,
these are the ways and manners
    of dervishes.

The ascetic's eyes are set on heaven,
    contemplating palaces promised there.
The niche of *faqr* and *fana*
    is the paradise of dervishes.

From pre- to post-eternity,
    the atoms of the universe spin
out of longing for
    a glance from dervishes.

From whom are you seeking alchemy?
    You will never find it.
Alchemy is only possible
    through service to dervishes.

Do not be proud of yourself;
    do not mock dervishes.
Everything other than God is cut off
    by the exclusive love of the dervishes.

One can never describe
....or define dervishes,
yet all that you see in the world
....bears witness to dervishes.

Nurbakhsh, why are you
....again speaking of dervishes?
Speech itself is left shamefaced
....in trying to adequately praise the dervishes.

MY LORD

I am he who cannot be contained
    by the narrow kingdom of the world;
my home is beyond the sun and moon
    that hang in the sky.

I have sold creation and everything therein
    for a grain of barley,
for the sphere of forms and images
    is not my place.

Wayfarers have left
    no footprints behind;
when I look closely
    there is no trace of mine.

No one is a stranger
    in this realm;
whomever I approach
    is known to me from afar.

In the entire world I find no trace
    other than the Friend's;
wherever I look,
    I see my Lord.

At the gathering called
    the banquet of love
I summon now
    the travelers on the mystical path.

At dawn, with the ear
    of awareness,
I heard God's herald proclaim:
    "Nurbakhsh, your light is for Me."

SEARCHING FOR LOVE

My soul has detached itself
    from the people of the world
and is at peace,
    away from the chatter of this world.

My heart was a servant of people
    for so many years;
having suffered much,
    it now shies away from them.

For a lifetime my heart has been occupied
    with the pursuit of love,
but I found no one
    who could appreciate love.

Truly I discovered
    that mankind is full of evil,
and he has not picked a single flower of goodness
    from the garden of humanity.

Every moment he dreams up and imagines
    something different,
rather than listening
    to what he is being told.

He does not honor his vows,
    and for this reason
each one sets off somewhere
    to follow his own desires.

I saw the person who had given
    the hand of friendship to Nurbakhsh
hiding in a corner
    with his hands withdrawn.

THE BLIND ALLEY OF LIFE

The thread of "I" and "you"[1] can be
    severed from the world.
O swift-winged bird,
    the cage of the body is breakable.

O idle babbler,
    what is this delay?
This blind alley of life is
    no place to settle.

Pass from this world;
    there is nothing to see here,
for it is but an empty promise,
    a broken cup.

Your selfishness is the bait,
    your imagination the snare.
How weary your body and soul are
    from this bait and snare!

At rest is the Sufi who has become freed
    from the fetters of "I" and "you."
Yes, the way of safety is to become
    free from these fetters.

The bird of the heart, finding the wings
    and feathers of aspiration,
flew from its roof,
    as it knew it should soar.

When Nurbakhsh separated
    from all of creation,
he saw that a bond with "other than the Truth"
    should not be made.

FOR YOU

Don't be so coy — the house of my heart
    is a home for You;
whatever is, and whatever is not —
    it's all for You.

The bewitching look of Your drunken eye
    has stolen my heart;
like a bird, my heart is ever
    yearning for You.

O beautiful idol, You are more alluring
    than any flower.
Come back! Like a rosebush, my eyelashes
    have withered without You.

Liberated from time and space,
    I am your servant;
observe how the king of the beautiful
    becomes a beggar before You.

The world is dead without love.
    Life is found only
in the glorious shadow cast by Your phoenix;[1]
    this grace is from You.

You've caused such mayhem that wherever I go
    over the course of time
all I hear from everyone is the havoc
    that has been wrought by You.

In pledging his life to Your drunken
    narcissus eye,
Nurbakhsh came to know that
    whoever has a heart is afflicted by You.

LOVE'S COMMOTION

From the heart of every atom
    I hear, "the Friend, the Friend."
So don't even see the atom,
    for there is really nothing but Him.

The song of reason and love
    comes from a single Reed Player's breath;
while intellect is engaged in discussion and debate,
    love creates commotion.

It is the Beloved Himself who is searching
    and seeking in love's marketplace,
while the poor lover has become
    disgraced in the town.

I asked the master,
    "If the path of Truth is but one,
why then all these embellishments?"
    "Merely for color and scent," he said.

If you wish to behold His face
    seek an eye capable of seeing God,
for fickle desire is a vagabond,
    wandering every moment to a different door.

The ocean's outward manifestations
    are called bubble and wave,
yet in reality it is all water,
    whether droplet, stream or sea.

The Beloved is the Bestower of light;
    ask Him to lend you sight
so you may see clearly
    His splendor displayed everywhere.

FROM HIM

All these wondrous forms in the world
    are from Him.
This joyful and embodied imagination
    is also from Him.

Eyes are from Him, light from Him,
    the power of sight is from Him.
Seeing and the seen are from Him,
    our insight into this world is entirely from Him.

Resolve is from Him, strength from Him,
    action too is from Him.
The path is from Him, coming and going,
    every step and each arrival, all are from Him.

Generosity and being are from Him,
    cause and effect are from Him.
Joy and grief are from Him,
    the wound is from Him, the salve too from Him.

The cage and the shackles are from Him,
    bait and snare are from Him.
The bird is from Him, the garden from Him,
    the high- and low-keyed melodies also are from Him.

I am from Him, home is from Him,
    service and aspiration are from Him.
Wealth is from Him, the generosity of hand from Him,
    the warmth of the hearth is from Him.

All of creation subsists through the aspiration
    of love.
The binding of atom with atom and all the particles
    of the cosmos are from Him.

Nurbakhsh, from whom
    is your warmhearted breath?
If you listen I will tell you,
    this, too, is from Him.

THE DWELLING OF THE DERVISH

The nest of existence
    is the dwelling of the dervish;
he exists for the world,
    and the world exists for him.

When he decides to leave this abode,
    he will reside in a place
that is the realm
    of his own annihilation.

With no name or trace
    he will travel there,
to behold his Lord manifest
    everywhere in that realm.

His discerning eyes
    see no strangers;
wherever he looks
    everyone is his friend.

When, like a reed-pipe,
    his heart is emptied of "I" and "we,"[1]
the Reed Player's breath blows through him,
    "I am the Truth."[2]

No one knows the dervish
    but God;
his beginning is God,
    and God is his end.

O Nurbakhsh, you have raised high
    the banner of the dervish in the world;
this action, too,
    is from the purity of the dervish.

THE COMMANDER OF CREATION

O You Whose essence is free from
    everything that exists:
You are beyond measure and description;
    You transcend everything that is.

Whoever described You
    has erred.
You are outside the bounds of description
    and more sublime than everything that is.

The temporal can't define
    the eternal.
You are beyond us
    and rise above everything that is.

I am non-being, while You are the True Being;
    I will say no more.
You are hidden from sight,
    yet apparent in everything that is.

You settled in my eyes,
    then with Your eyes I saw
You are manifest
    in everything that is.

You are the ruler of the realm of possibilities
    and the commander of creation.
You are all-knowing; Yours is the power
    over everything that is.

You are not a drop
    to seek the company of the Ocean.
O Nurbakhsh,
    He is free from everything that is.

ALL EXISTENCE

This existence of yours derives
    from another source;
everything noteworthy in the world exists
    through Him.

There is no sign of "other than God"
    in the realm of Unity;
through His radiance every trace appears
    in full beauty.

How long will you remain captive
    in the prison of the self?
Break the ego's cage
    if you are artful enough!

Why boast of your intellect, which
    in a lifetime yields nothing?
Cling to love, for it alone bears
    worthwhile fruit!

Without love, there would be no trace
    of this world's existence.
All existence, whether verdant or barren, is manifest
    through love's intervention.

This self you rely on is
    but a veil;
remove the veil of your self
    and you will see the Other.

The light that bestowed life upon
    all the heavens
comes from the bewitching breath of the One
    with a transforming glance.

THE FIRE TEMPLE OF LOVE

We bring good tidings to those
    without news.
The news we bring is from Him;
    we ourselves have nothing to say.

After Unity has staked Its claim,
    there is a fire temple
in the realm of the heart,
    with its flame still blazing.

Our retreat is renowned
    the world over,
for enamored people
    can be found here.

Since we know how to sacrifice our heads
    and break the self,
let everyone know
    that we do indeed possess an art.

In the garden of loving-kindness,
    we are a barren and leafless tree.
Only through our burning
    shall we bear fruit.

It was our heart's blood
    that gushed from our eyes.
Therefore, our eyes are inspiring
    and keen in perception.

If Nurbakhsh is forgiven,
    it is because
there is a burning fire in his heart,
    which is intimate, passionate and warm.

GOD AND LOVE

We have no dealings with anyone
    but the Friend.
The lover is not enslaved
    by images and forms.

Are you still parading your existence
    before the Beloved's eyes?
Then your love has proven
    to be worthless.

How could a lovesick one
    complain of pain?
Be gone, O false claimant,
    for you don't truly pine for the Friend.

You are not a lover
    if you are settled and secure.
Indeed, he whose head is not hung
    from the gallows is not victorious.[1]

Better to spend this life
    with wine and the Beloved,
for one cannot depend
    on this transient realm.

I saw that in the lover's eyes
    God is love.
And I say there is no better maxim
    than this.

Never, never did my turbulent heart
    find calm.
Clearly, for the poor lover
    there is no rest.

Nurbakhsh has fallen
    into a trap;
he has no thought of escaping
    and no feet of his own with which to do so.

THE LANTERN OF LOVE

Wine is forbidden to those not languishing
    half drunk at the banquet of the soul.
This is a decree of the master of the holy fire,[1]
    not a religious doctrine.

Whoever follows us on the feet
    of surrender and contentment
is not excused if he finds fault
    with what we do.

To whom should I say this? No one has
    enough enthusiasm for traversing the path,
though the path of love is easy
    and the goal not far.

Put aside cleverness and sobriety,
    be full of yearning!
The secrets of the heart-ravishers
    are not concealed from lovers.

Many are near, yet in truth are far,
    far away from us;
many are far away but
    not really separated from us.

In the darkness of multiplicity
    what guide is there but love?
With the lantern of love there is
    no gloom in the pitch black night.

O Nurbakhsh, do not reveal the secrets
    of the *rendan* to the pious ascetics —
those captains have no light
    at the bows of their ships.

YEARNING FOR YOU

There is no path
> without Your tracks and footprints.
There are no eyes
> that do not yearn to see You everywhere.

In the hermitage, shrine, idol-temple
> and Magian cloister — there is nowhere
that is without news
> of Your lovely face.

It is right that all particles exclaim
> "I am the Truth,"[1]
since there is no trace in existence
> that does not come from You.

Every heart, sober or drunk,
> has a way to You.
There is no door leading there that is not open
> to the people of the world, thanks to You.

In the rose garden of Your beauty
> there is such a vibrant commotion!
Every flower, herb and fruit
> can be found there.

The intellect is lost and stupefied
> on Your path,
but there is no art that love
> has not mastered in Your court.

Nurbakhsh has left everyone and sits silently
> in a corner, for there is no nook
that is not full of clamor and commotion
> because of You.

THERE IS NAUGHT...

Nothing but the light of God
    is apparent.
At every place and in every direction
    only He is manifest.

He remains as He was
    in the beginning.
Other than Absolute Being,
    nothing in the world truly exists.

What appears to your eyes is but
    an imaginary form.
Don't rely on this fantasy,
    for to do so is futile.

Abandon other skills, and seek only
    that of love.
No other skill in the world
    is worthwhile.

Of all the opportunities in life,
    only the one presented by love is fruitful.
Of all the seeds that could be sown in the ground,
    only the seed of love bears fruit.

Each moment, every particle of the world
    comes alive through love.
How can eyes that lack true vision
    perceive this?

If the True Beloved bestows light
    upon you,
the world will have no news
    of your existence.

NOTHING OTHER THAN YOU

The world and everything in it is nothing
    other than You;
the hidden face of all that's apparent is nothing
    other than You.

You appear to me as the life force behind
    all that exists;
this is not mere belief — I know for certain, there is nothing
    other than You.

The fantasy of "I" and "you"[1] is nothing but
    a childish dream;
when thoughts pass away there is nothing
    other than You.

All lines and patterns representing
    the visible realm
spring from a single point drawn by You; there is nothing
    other than You.

Seen through the eyes of the people of the heart,
    each wave of this infinite ocean
is just a manifestation of You, for there is nothing
    other than You.

The mystics have come to know You through
    Your own eyes;
they have confirmed that there is nothing
    other than You.

I am radiant due to Your bestowal of light — I see that,
    though everything appears to have a body and soul,
in reality there is nothing
    other than You.

THE PAVILION OF UNITY

My heart's passion for You allows
    for no other desire;
it pines only to be sacrificed
    in Your cross-like curls.

Moses, bewildered by the fire burning
    in the Sinai of my heart,
does not even hope
    for an ember.[1]

Once we know You, we cannot know
    anyone else;
in fact, when I look closely, there is no one
    other than You.

In the field of Oneness I've set up
    my pavilion of Unity.
Thank heavens! No mullahs or militia
    are allowed there.

I am lost in the realm of bewilderment,
    and in that desert
there are no tracks from any caravan
    and no sound of the camels' bells.

O worthless ascetic! Stop your
    pretentious display!
A fly does not belong
    in the realm of the phoenix.

The light that is bestowed
    upon the firebrand *rendan*
will not illuminate the path
    for every useless rascal.

MYSTERIES OF THE HEART

There is no heart
    that cannot be set alight by His rays.
There is no soul
    that cannot burn in His fire.

The fabric of reason
    is of no use —
a heart torn by love
    can't be mended.

To gamble and lose to the beautiful ones
    is gain indeed —
the commodity of love can't
    be hoarded.

With his intellect the scholar
    can't comprehend our world —
a hundred thanks that the heart's mysteries
    can't be learned!

O pretender, have shame
    before God!
Counterfeit goods
    can't be sold to everyone!

He can't be called the "soul"
    for He is the Bestower of soul to the world.
He can't be called "body"
    for that Spirited One is not a body.

His sun-like face
    bestows light to the heart.
Truly, there is no heart
    that cannot be set alight by His rays.

THE SUFI'S RETREAT

In the heart of the selfless there is room
    only for the Beloved;
in the Sufi's retreat there is no room
    for anyone else.

When the space of the heart
    fills with love,
no stranger can be seen,
    there is no room for others.

O mullah, in the banquet of madness
    don't boast of your intellect;
in the circle of the drunk,
    there is no room for the sober.

The lover's book contains no mention
    of states and stations,
or talk of *adab*; there is no room
    for secrets.

In the religion of the people of the heart,
    litany and prayer express self-existence;
where no desire exists, there is no room
    for insistence.

In that lane where heads roll,
    there is no "I" and "we";[1]
a chief would be out of place,
    there is no room for a commander.

Light will be bestowed upon you the moment
    you cease to exist;
in the darkness of "I" and "we"
    there is no room for light.

THE STORY OF LOVE

The world and everything therein
    should not be overvalued;
whoever becomes God's friend
    is not concerned with other than Him.

The mullah heard the story of love
    and called it mere fiction;
I told the same story of love to the mountain
    and saw its heart grow restless with agitation.

A heart that does not love
    is neither pure nor sincere.
How could one who has no beloved
    know anything about fidelity and love?

Why trust the pledge
    of worldly people?
A slave of caprice is not constant enough
    to keep his word.

The intellect promised me
    an earthly kingdom,
but it does not know that a runaway heart
    places no hope in the world.

Ask the selfish, ignorant mullah,
    why all these boastful airs?
The ways of arrogance and ostentation
    are nothing to be proud of.

On the path of fate
    Nurbakhsh fell into a trap
from which he is neither willing
    nor able to escape.

THE WORLD OF LOVE AND REVELRY

The world of love and revelry
        knows no security or rest;
its pain, sorrow and affliction
        are without wailing and sighs.

It is a wondrous realm,
        beyond both worlds.
Space can't contain it;
        it has no boundaries, no shores.

In that realm "we" and "I"[1]
        are never mentioned.
There is no wisdom or intellect,
        neither speech nor exposition.

Whoever is familiar with that realm
        becomes estranged from self;
wherever he goes, he is a stranger,
        without trace or name.

His heart is freed from all things;
        indeed he is unconscious of self.
In this place, the thought of being
        or non-being brings only loss.

The madman of God's path
        is considered the master of intellect,
and though he is the very soul of the soul,
        he has no concern for the soul.

Since Nurbakhsh gambled
        and lost everything in love,
he has no expectation of friendship
        from anyone.

REPUTATION FOR MADNESS

With every breath my sweetheart
    displays Himself in a different form.
By God! There should be limits
    to such enchanting ways!

Fidelity has stitched
    the pages of loving-kindness;
see how firmly the book of love
    is bound with faithfulness.

Layli avoided Majnun
    because she heard
that the poor lover was renowned
    in the desert of madness.

The realm of non-existence
    has both a tower and a gate,[1]
made of the heads of the exalted ones
    and the hearts of seekers.

O Nurbakhsh, the mystery you have spoken of
    is resolved for me now:
with every breath, my sweetheart
    displays Himself in a different form.

LOVE'S EXISTENCE

From love, existence has come to possess
    a wondrous fervor and music —
the heart of every seemingly worthless atom
    contains God.

Not only the dust dwellers
    stricken with grief for Him have purity of heart —
wherever love pitches its tent,
    that place becomes serene.

Be a servant of the master of the Magi,
    for in the realm of *baqa*
only those are truly alive who have received from him
    the sanction of *fana*.

Abandon self-worship, my friend,
    for no one with
any trace of self shall enter
    the presence of the Friend.

The tavern's retreat
    is a safe place indeed,
with healing water
    and a rejuvenating atmosphere.

One can't receive a cup from the cupbearer
    through mere desire —
only those with true yearning
    are granted this wine.

Nurbakhsh, stop seeking a remedy.
    Be at rest,
for this pain of ours
    has no cure.

THE SONG OF UNITY

Once again, the minstrel played
    the song of Unity,
liberating us by love
    from any need of both worlds.

Thank God that my restless heart
    has passed from itself
and found the path
    to the tavern.

O mullah, don't say that the religion
    of wine-worshipers is a different creed;
the cupbearer performs the funeral rite
    for the deceased drunkard.

That one who, in the guise of friendship,
    set the trap of deception
in the district of purity
    is a stranger.

Whoever severed his bond with us and left the path
    was given to illusion;
he acted fairly to leave
    and set out for the realm of his imagination.

The lover who was steeped in neediness
    turned away in disregard
and vigorously ignored
    everything other than the Friend.

On the Beloved's path
    Nurbakhsh is excused
for having gone a long way
    and spoken at length.

REASSESSMENT OF LOVE

Once again, I will reassess
    my love for You;
I will inform everyone
    of my view.

I will extinguish
    the fire of separation in my breast;
I will put out of my head
    the thought of union with You.

I will erase the words
    "I and the Beloved"
and make "love" an epic
    told beyond all horizons.

Through friendship with You,[1]
    I will shut my eyes to all else
and gaze on Your face
    with Your eyes.

I will break the head and feet of seeking
    with the rock of zeal,
and travel everywhere
    with You on Your feet.

I will evacuate
    the realm of "I" and "we"[2]
and come to Your quarters
    dead drunk.

O Nurbakhsh,
    I will inform you about yourself
so that you will stop telling the others
    what else you will do.

THOSE WITHOUT LOVE AND PURITY[1]

One can't rely on those
    who have no purity and love;
one should not let oneself be ridiculed[2]
    by every aimless fool.

Avoid entering the tavern
    of the Magi for as long as you can,
but once you set foot there,
    don't question anything.

No one has ever arrived
    at the final destination,
yet one should not stop striving
    on the way to this goal.

In that banquet
    where one can't tell beggar from king,
one cannot speak of "up" and "down"
    or "we" and "you."

Never claim the title of "dervish"
    and "Sufi" for yourself,
for in this valley of bewilderment
    one must be without "I" and "you."[3]

Don't take love for a toy;
    don't laugh at the lovers.
In this arithmetic
    one cannot add two and two so simply.

O Nurbakhsh, once again
    you have spoken of love —
this is the pain
    that nothing can cure.

ONE CANNOT

In God's work one cannot
    question anything;
one cannot talk of "I" and "you"[1]
    on the spiritual path.

Though we are the people
    of loyalty and purity,
one cannot remain serene with those
    who are disloyal.

O expert on the canon law,
    we know you well —
you cannot deceive a sincere Sufi
    with your hypocrisy.

Be a reformer of yourself,
    for in the school of integrity
one cannot invite others to rectitude
    through faulty means.

O hypocrites, while worshiping
    all these idols
one cannot call out,
    "God! God!"

As God has granted the chance
    of a few more days,
one cannot continue for years
    with highway robbery.

We heard Nurbakhsh saying
    to himself,
"One cannot be oppressive and cruel
    to God's creation."

THE WAYWARD INTELLECT

He who was parading his "I" and "we"[1]
    in a hundred different ways yesterday,
today I saw crying,
    "O my Lord, O my God!"

I said, "Be thankful
    for God's concealment;
He could have exposed you
    for your shameless stubbornness."

The wayward intellect,
    known for infamy and ill-repute,
was mocking
    and shaming love.

But in the end the harvest
    of its existence was scattered to the winds,
although in private
    it would deny this fact.

In madness love erased
    the book of knowledge,
while the man of reason watched
    from outside love's circle.

Love's method
    is total silence.
Otherwise, its eloquence of speech
    would cause an uproar.

Those slain by love
    have no desire to talk or be heard.
Otherwise, Nurbakhsh, too,
    would have created a commotion.

THE TORRENT

The torrent of the path
    brings the mind to a boil;[1]
the ocean of *fana*
    causes oblivion and quietness.

In the assembly of the people of mystical states
    the only speech is silence;
it is the banquet of multiplicity
    that fosters whispering.

We have drained a goblet,
    and fallen eternally drunk.
What other wine
    could cause such a stupor?

It is no wonder
    that we have forgotten our selves.
Yes, the thought of the Friend
    causes forgetfulness.

In pre-eternity,
    this was my lot:
to sit always by a vat
    of intoxicating wine.

The dream of love
    reveals the face of Truth,
while the intellect slumbers like a rabbit:
    open-eyed but fast asleep.

Out of yearning,
    Nurbakhsh has composed this poem,
for the torrent of the path
    brings the mind to a boil.

THE HUMAN PREY

How can I resolve this problem of my heart
    when the Beloved's demand is so difficult?
Before telling me anything about Himself
    first He makes me die.

The cupbearer won't pour the wine of love
    into the heart's cup
unless one vows to renounce
    both religion and reason.

No one is sober
    in the tavern of Unity;
there, no drunkard will find fault
    with other drunks.

Those afflicted with pain for Him,
    never search for a cure.
His destitute beggar will never find
    the comfort of a home.

In the land of lovers,
    no enraptured one will gain subsistence
unless he first receives the command
    for his own banishment and *fana*.

We saw that the Beloved was Himself the compensation
    for those slain by love;
that is not to say that Nurbakhsh
    will not demand a price from those slain by him.

WITHOUT LOVE

Without love
    one's breath is empty
and one cannot set foot
    near any beloved.

When the nightingale of love
    shed its feathers,
the rose relocated
    amid thorns and thickets.

When a heart is not
    drunk with the Beloved,
whatever it says
    is out of raw desire.

Every time that the bird-like heart
    fluttered its wings
inside the cage, it was
    out of joy and ecstasy.

The moment love arrived
    at my door,
it pushed aside the display
    of the intellect.

Once love became the ruler of
    the heart's realm,
it cut off the way of the mufti[1]
    and his enforcers everywhere.

Nurbakhsh's heart
    was lost in love,
as he constantly breathed
    in remembrance of Him.

ONE WHO KNOWS GOD

Whoever knows God
    has no concern for other than Him.

Whoever is afflicted by Him
    knows God to be the cure for his pain.

Self-worship is not God-worship —
    this truth is our motto.

Be non-existent, so you may truly be;
    the Absolute Being is clearly God alone.

When the drop ceases to see itself, it becomes the ocean;
    fana comes first, then *baqa*.

There is no dispute among *rendan*;
    whoever becomes a *rend* is pure.

The Bestower of light to all creation is One,
    though He may be reflected in a thousand mirrors.

THE CANE OF HERESY

Don't wonder how it will turn out —
reason will surrender to madness.

All awareness will leave my head;
my heart will bleed at Your hands.

If love were to rattle the chains
the age-old cosmos would be humbled.

Your flirtation brings turmoil to all,
bewitching both drunken and sober.

Whoever sees Your *alef*[1]-like loftiness will bend down
like *dal*[2] — no — will sink even lower, like *nun*.[3]

The banner of Your love shall be raised high;
the cane that accuses of heresy shall be cast down.[4]

Nurbakhsh sat by himself, away from everyone;
now, he shall leave himself, too.

THE TAVERN DOOR

Only by the sword of love
    will my heart be torn to shreds
and my eyes become
    fountains of my heart's blood.

Our hearts cannot contain
    anything but His fire.
Without His Qur'an-like face
    my heart cannot be split into thirty parts.[1]

I am a lover in a wretched state,
    so don't imagine that I am idle.
Whoever is a lover
    is never without work.

He who has become a Majnun due to Layli's face
    will not go insane;[2]
one who is lost in His district
    will not become an aimless wanderer.

The *rend* will not remove his lips
    from the goblet's rim,
while the sheikh,[3] in his sobriety,
    will never taste wine.

The one enraptured by His face
    will be firm in love;
he journeys within himself,
    and will not become a vagabond.

By the pure love of God
    the lover is innocent,
and the soul within him
    will never become a tyrant.[4]

If light is bestowed
    it is because that enraptured one
will never stop waiting by
    the tavern door.

THE DISTRAUGHT HEART

Once again my distraught heart
    has contracted in pain,
but speaking brings relief
    and heals the heartache.

Once we were free of pain,
    the sorrow of the heart a stranger to us.
Then a frenzied madness set in
    and the stranger became an intimate.

Unity had set us free from concern
    about having more or less.
Then from the bottle of multiplicity
    sorrow was poured into the heart's mouth.

In the banquet of lovers
    our way is silence;
the lover who breathes a word
    is imperfect in love.

O ruinous love,
    you devastated me and said,
"Whoever is slain by me
    is of the rank of Adam."[1]

O love, in your presence there is safety,
    while in your district there is blame.
Whoever keeps company with you
    becomes steeped in suffering and grief.

If now and then Nurbakhsh
    remembers You with a sigh,
it is because every moment
    he receives grace from You.

THE CRAZED HEART

How I sacrificed my soul for Him,
    but my soul's Beloved did not come!
That Breaker of promises
    never came to fill the cup.

In His district, I lost my heart
    and religion —
still my Sorcerer never returned
    to end the tale.

The preacher gave me advice,
    but, alas, he did not know
that the manners of the wise
    cannot be expected from the mad.

I burned up in His flame-like face,
    yet no one knew —
like a *rend* I endured burning
    even a moth could not.

Not until we smashed
    the cup and the pitcher at His feet
did that drunken Heart-ravisher
    come to the tavern.

Not until He heard
    the proclamation of "I am the Truth"[1]
from every idol's lips, did the heart's Conqueror[2]
    leave the Kaaba for the idol-temple.

My bird-like heart was in search of the Hunter
    with all its soul;
if it entered the trap
    it was not for the sake of the bait.

When He bestowed light on me,
    I lost control of my heart —
and that heart
    never returned home.

THE PRAYER NICHE OF SUPPLICATION

The one who was made
    the prayer niche[1] of supplication
has been a confidant of the secret
    from the first day of creation.

To hide the beauty of the Truth
    from the creation,
a hundred different illusory forms
    were created.

Some people were created for joy
    and pleasure,
others for burning
    and melting.

The mystic was created for non-being,
    helplessness and humility,
the mullah for asceticism
    and prayer.

To clear away "I" and "we"[2]
    on the way of love,
a rising and falling path
    was created.

To turn a traveler towards
    the Kaaba of his goal,
the *shur*, *nava*, *turk* and *hijaz*[3] melodies
    were created.

I know Nurbakhsh
    is kind to his foes,
though it is for kindness to friends
    that he was created.

LOVE'S ASCENSION

The burnt up ones are occupied with flames and smoke;[1]
    the cupbearer and wine drinkers are huddled together.
The hearts in their breasts — vats of wine bubbling but silent —
    are like the world-revealing cup of Jamshid.[2]

Like moths, all are circling the candle's flame;
    they are blissful, without words or desire.
The fire of Unity blazed up and consumed their awareness
    of "I" and "we,"[3] which is not allowed near.

O cupbearer, the tavern is running out of wine
    though seemingly wine-worshipers are few.
Pass around the goblet, for in this gathering
    there are no jinn or angels; all are children of Adam.

All are thoroughly drunk and unconscious,
    freed from thoughts about profit and loss.
None among this throng is sober;
    these are the wayfarers of love.

In one direction, with one breath, unified, all are intermingled,
    intermixed, and dissolved into one another.
They are effaced from themselves, so only the One is manifest;
    now all subsist through the One.

Even that has passed from view;
    they are unconscious, traceless and intangible.
No sign at all of anyone can be found;
    they are beyond this relative realm.

Purer than heart, lighter than spirit,
    they travel without feet and steps.
Grasp the hems of their robes, Nurbakhsh,
    for they are a salve for the wounds of a burned heart.

GOD'S HOUSE

Those filled with the pain of longing for You
    do not think about a cure;
they have given up both heart and religion,
    and sit here without "I" and "we."[1]

Your lovers come
    by the way of fidelity,
and with purity
    sit at Your doorway.

In the royal court of Your grace,
    the beggars at Your door
sit with their needs satisfied
    and their hearts joyful.

Your needy ones have no regard
    for existence and the world;
they sit in Your sanctuary
    without provisions.

When Your wine-worshipers
    encircle Your vat,
they sit, goblet in hand,
    without asking *why* or *how*.

Life[2] is not worth a grain of barley[3]
    for those afflicted by Your love.
How then could they sit
    hoping for a cure?

In God's house, it is impossible
    for the men of God
to sit inattentive to Him, like you,
    O pretenders!

The retreat of the *rendan*
    bestows light to the heavens.
All sit in remembrance of God,
    facing God.

THE DIVINE REED PLAYER

Clear the way
    so that those with self-existence
can leave
    and the annihilated ones can enter!

The former remain slaves
    and victims of themselves;
the latter have pawned themselves in
    God's sanctuary.

Those without love
    remain deprived of the Truth —
having sown no seeds,
    what can they reap?

Emptied of self,
    like the reed pipe,
Sufis listen
    to the Divine Reed Player.

The clever, though they boast
    about their intellects,
run around in despair
    in every direction.

The mystics who are unaware of self
    have become
oblivious to what is outmoded
    and detached from what is fashionable.

If lovers ever revealed
    the secret,
intellectuals would bite their nails
    in bewilderment.

Those radiant beauties
    who speak of love
bestow light
    wherever they go.

THE TREASURE CHEST OF MYSTERIES

I remember bygone days
    when my breast was the treasure chest of mysteries.
The soul was fervently occupied with love,
    and the hands were held out in supplication.

The heart pined for the Beloved
    and was steeped in need.
He was there, with beauty
    and purity and the play and teasing of love.

There was hope and desire for union with the Friend.
    From night till dawn my eyes
were fixed on His door
    and it was open all the while.

How drunkenly
    I passed my days,
with goblet in hand,
    listening to the melody of the lute.

There was no separation,
    no suffering or unfaithfulness,
and out of fidelity
    the Beloved was kind to my heart.

There was only the image of His visage
    in the core of the heart;
the soul, through its rapt attention to His face,
    was in perpetual prayer.

I never regret
    that those pleasant dreams have ended,
for illusion was the chamberlain
    of the Truth.

O Nurbakhsh, the discussion
    about truth and illusion
does not remain now
    though it began long ago.

I only meant to tell the story
    and the state of the heart
when burning and contentment
    were its intimates.

During those years,
    freed from the worry of the world,
the Mahmud-like soul
    was captivated by the beauty of Ayaz.[1]

I said to myself, "Those were happy days."
    Hearing this, my heart said,
"Don't conceal that
    our affair burned us away in tribulation."

YEARNING TO SEE YOU

Your Beauty had no buyer
    but You;
You were the sole customer — no one
    was in the marketplace but You.

You fashioned a mirror
    to see Your own beauty,
You saw there was no one yearning
    to behold it but You.

You made the caravan of creation
    appear from non-existence,
yet in that multiplicity
    no one was there but You.

Your Being raised a commotion
    like the trumpet blaring of resurrection;
we discovered that all was just imagined —
    there was really no one but You.

All the atoms of the cosmos are roaming
    in the sleep of non-existence;
no one is awake
    in existence but You.

With the eye of my soul
    I saw this truth:
since pre-eternity there has been
    no one but You.

Nurbakhsh saw that
    from pre- to post-eternity
there was never anyone manifest
    in existence but You.

WITHOUT YOU

In pre-eternity no face existed
    other than Your beautiful countenance,
and there was no direction to travel
    except towards You.

You fell in love
    with Your own face,
for there was no beloved
    as lovely as You.

You saw plainly Your face
    in Your own mirror,
untainted by tresses
    and curls.

Even now, there is no beloved
    separate from You.
Without You the world would
    lack color and fragrance.

The image of existence came into being
    through the curve of Your eyebrows;
if You didn't exist, there would never be
    any endeavor or seeking.

There is nothing other than You
    in all manifestations of being;
no idol or temple would have existed
    without You.

The bestower of light is none
    other than You,
and this "I" and "you"[1] is nothing
    other than a pointless commotion.

BEWITCHING EYES

My drunken Beloved stepped out
 from Her house;
my frenzied heart became
 chained in madness.

Thousands of bewitching glances
 darted from Her eyes,
and the hearts of the people had gathered,
 desiring to fall under their spell.

Creation was unable
 to fathom Her steps;
next to Her grandeur
 existence seemed despicable and disgraced.

Myriad suns and moons
 were bewildered on Her path;
heavenly spheres in countless numbers
 followed Her steed on foot.

Her *alef*[1]-like loftiness
 raised the commotion of resurrection;
the back of the universe bent over
 and collapsed like *nun*.[2]

Every nimble-footed runner
 had fallen over by the wayside;
the head of every exalted man
 was bent low.

I, a needy, wretched lover,
 was bewildered:
why was the Unique Sweetheart
 revealing Herself to all?

In a state of rapture
 Nurbakhsh was crying out
and his heart's blood
 was dripping from his eye.

WHOEVER BECOMES NOTHING WILL REACH GOD

Whoever becomes nothing
    will reach God —
when a wave disappears it merges
    with the ocean.

Stamp out yourself and
    become Him —
the drop loses its identity when it
    dissolves into the sea.

The one who forgets himself
    from head to toe
will have the good fortune
    to complete the path.

Love's vast ocean can be achieved
    through self-effacement —
the one who has no place can reach
    the ultimate destination.

Whoever becomes hidden
    from the eyes of the people
will have his own truth-seeing eyes
    opened by God.

Annihilate the idol of
    self-worship —
only then will the Truth
    be revealed to you.

Listen to Nurbakhsh with your heart
    and soul —
whoever becomes nothing
    will reach God.

THE CANDLE OF BEING

People sting me, but for me
    that sting becomes a salve;
this, too, is forgotten
    and passes from my mind.

When my Illuminator, out of compassion,
    shows me His face,
the candle of my being
    becomes snuffed out at once.

"Pay attention," He says,
    "For I will enter through your door."
But when He arrives,
    all sense leaves my head.

"Speak up!" He tells me.
    "I will hear what you have to say."
But my heart and soul
    only listen to His words.

"Why don't You remove the covering
    from Your face?" I ask.
"Your 'why' itself becomes a veil,"
    He replies.

Wait, O Cupbearer,
    there is no need for wine!
The heart is falling in a stupor
    from Your intoxicating eyes.

Nurbakhsh, as long as you are free from
    the thought of other than Him,
people may sting you, but for you
    that sting becomes a salve.

AT THE TAVERN DOOR

We are here at the tavern door,
    awaiting the Beloved's wish;
our only desire
    is whatever that Sweetheart wants.

A hundred thanks that we were set free
    from the tarnish of multiplicity!
Now, in the realm of Unity,
    what could the awakened heart want?

In the tavern, we are joyful
    and without desire;
there is a burning sigh in our breasts —
    what does it want?

In quest of the Beloved,
    my heart bled in suffering and my soul departed;
that cunning Heart-Ravisher —
    what more can She want?

Having abandoned reason,
    we are bewildered and drunk;
from drunkards
    what could the sensible, sober man want?

If slandered, we will not be offended,
    but only wonder
what that immature, ignorant slanderer
    could want.

Whether light is bestowed or not
    there is no worry;
our only desire is
    whatever that Sweetheart wants.

THE SEASON FOR ANEMONES

The turn of the ascetics has passed;
    the era of lovers has come.
The moon of the Occident is eclipsed;
    the sun of the Orient has come.

O novice fire-worshipers, good news:
    the Magi covenant[1] is renewed.
Illusion has disappeared,
    and the time for realities has come.

You who are love-crazed,
    rejoice drunkenly:
play that sweet melody,[2]
    for good fortune has come.

The master of the tavern of love
    is heading to the vat again —
the time for *sama* and ecstasy is here;
    the sincere lover has come.

Lead the tavern haunters
    towards merriment.
Clap your hands and beat the tambourine;
    the appetite for mystical subtleties has come.

Autumn has passed
    and the spring breeze has wafted here.
The partridge is strutting about;
    the season for anemones has come.

Nurbakhsh hears the murmur,
    "Drink, drink. May it bring joy!"
Yes, the turn of the ascetics has passed;
    the era of lovers has come.

THE DECREE OF THE INTIMATES OF MYSTERIES

When you turn your faces towards
    the court of the One without need,
break first your talisman's spell
    of "I" and "we."[1]

Step beyond yourselves
    on the quest for the Friend;
you will attain the Truth
    if you avoid illusion.

Make your ablution with the pure water[2]
    of sincerity and truthfulness,
then perform the funeral prayer
    over your loveless and dead selves.

Be oblivious to everything
    but the Friend;
turn your backs on whomever is not
    privy to this work.

Remove your gaze from creation
    by remembering Him,
and avoid the throng
    of the loveless ones.

Success in this endeavor comes only
    through the Friend's grace;
proceed by relying upon the grace
    from that One Who grants success.

If, like Nurbakhsh,
    you seek the Beloved,
then perform the prayer of love according to
    the decree of the intimates of mysteries.

LOVE CRAZED

From love for You,
    I am more crazed than any madman,
for in beauty You are more precious
    than any pearl.

Compared to conventional reason
    we are mad,
yet, in this world we are wiser
    than any sage.

Within my heart and soul, every breath
    I become more intimate with You.
Yet I see myself more alien to You
    than any stranger.

Do you know why I see the Truth
    manifest with the soul's eye?
It is because I saw that "other than the Truth"
    is more of a fable than any fiction.

We sacrificed our heart and soul,
    offering the self as the price,
for in our eyes You were lovelier
    than any other beloved.

I fell into the trap of the pre-eternal hunter,
    bewildered until post-eternity.
Now, my bird-like heart is more homeless
    than any nestless bird.

O Candle of the gathering of the people of heart,
    O Bestower of inner light to physical forms,
I burn in Your fire more ardently
    than any moth.

THE BASIS OF CREATION

Without love, the world is a tribulation, altogether,
a place of affliction and disappointment, altogether.

Whoever is unacquainted with love
is a stranger to us, altogether.

Love is the basis of creation,
through which everything exists, altogether.

Without love, life is empty and meaningless,
a senseless farce, altogether.

A heart not burning from love's sorrow
contains only lust and desire, altogether.

If you're a person of heart, turn towards love;
a heart not burnt in love is a torment, altogether.

Nurbakhsh's heart spent a lifetime with love,
away from other than the Beloved, altogether.

THE OCEAN OF TRACELESSNESS

Drowned in the ocean of tracelessness,
>   I am oblivious to self,
with no concern for created beings.
>   What can trouble me now?

It has been a while since, through remembering Him,
>   I became estranged from self;
neither sting nor salve
>   can affect my state.

On the plane of madness
>   the heart has no creed.
Why then do these sensible people
>   still ask about my faith?

My Beloved plundered my heart and soul;
>   I now have nothing left.
So why still ask me
>   how much I possess?

If the Sweetheart plucks
>   the strings of madness,
it is only to soothe
>   my wounded heart.

O Nurbakhsh, the Beloved relentlessly
>   spilt our blood,
that He might say,
>   "I still remember the yearning dervishes."

HOLD ON!

Look everywhere for the knower
    of the path to God,
and hold on to the one who can
    snatch you from your self.

In the Friend's district, leave behind everything
    other than Him,
then in sincerity and contentment
    accept whatever comes.

Don't walk the path that does not lead
    to loving-kindness and fidelity;
follow the creed
    of love and purity.

Never seek out those
    who claim miracles;
grab onto those
    who are selfless.

If you spend your wealth and your life
    to attain the Friend,
then hang on to the rope
    of *faqr* and *fana*.

Keep away from those who are
    the prisoners of "I" and "we";[1]
stay with those who do not promote
    such selfishness.

Hear from Nurbakhsh
    this subtle advice:
seek love's remedy from
    the physician of love.

DON'T ACQUIRE!

Don't acquire a guide until you become
    a traveler on the path to God.
Don't go searching for God's love
    if you're still your own slave.

Don't ask us about the fable
    of heaven and hell;
don't seek any lesson from us other than
    the teaching of purity and loving-kindness.

Go to the place where there is
    the discourse of love and fidelity.
Avoid the deceit of the carnal self;
    don't associate with the followers of vain desires.

Choose as your companions the travelers
    on the path of the Truth.
Don't go chasing the followers
    of falsity and hypocrisy.

Dwell with the residents
    of the district of chivalry.
Don't ever ask the whereabouts
    of selfish people.

With valor let go of everything
    other than the Friend.
Don't choose a friend for yourself
    other than God.

Like Nurbakhsh, leave behind everything
    on the path to the Friend.
Endure the pain of love for the Friend
    and don't seek a remedy.

REPROACH IS WRONG

O Ravisher of my heart, I shall not ask You
    to unveil Your face;
rather grant me this favor —
    remove the veil from my eyes!

Wreck my self-seeing nature
    so You may behold Yourself in me.
What I mean is this:
    cast a glance at this hapless wretch!

No drop has ever seen the Ocean
    with its own eyes;
seek an eye from the Ocean,
    then see the water.

In the realm where they drink from
    the fountain of Your Essence,
snatch our being and cast it
    into the river of wine!

If you seek God,
    grasp and hold onto love,
but if you pursue vain desires,
    then keep looking every which way.

In the creed of God's *rendan*
    reproach is wrong;
unless you are a hypocrite,
    close your lips to all rebuke.

Since love has nothing to do
    with wakefulness or sleep,
O Nurbakhsh,
    drunkenly spread your bed!

THE SONG OF PRAISE[1]

Thank God the tavern door is still open,
    and the hearts of the *rendan* in the world
are still confidants
    of the divine mysteries.

The fire of wine gave our being
    to the winds of effacement,
yet our yearning heart
    still burns.

The taste for madness
    does not forbid the worship of wine;
the crazed heart
    is still allowed to follow this tradition.

So many tales fade
    from memory,
but the legend of Mahmud and Ayaz[2]
    remains etched on the seal of love.

O cupbearer, pass the wine!
    The Beloved is flirtatiously ignoring us,
for in our intoxication
    we are still conscious of our neediness.

Although the musician of our assembly
    is bereft of self,
the heart's ear is still captive
    to the melody of the lute.

From within the vat's heart,
    Nurbakhsh heard the call to prayer.
The mullah, however, was saying,
    "Wait, it's not yet the time to pray!"

THE BOASTFUL ARE NOT PRIVY TO THE PATH OF LOVING-KINDNESS

Wine worship is the way
    of the ocean-hearted, O friend,
and the game of love
    is the art of the perfected ones, O friend.

The soft and pampered
    are not admitted to the gathering of drunks;
proud airs and impatience
    are the way of intellectuals, O friend.

Idol breaking is the creed
    of the *rendan* alone;
idol worship is the religion
    of the futile, O friend.

The boastful are not privy
    to the path of loving-kindness;
our retreat is far removed
    from such unworthy ones, O friend.

Do not seek erudition and logic
    in the circle of the people of love;
those fables are taught
    only by the learned, O friend.

If you belong at our banquet
    then drink and be silent;
brawling in drunkenness
    is the manner of the ignorant, O friend.

Nurbakhsh drank vats of wine
    and still remained silent.
Whoever acts disgracefully in drinking
    lacks discipline,[1] O friend.

THE CREED OF THE *RENDAN*

Sacrifice your soul on the quest for the Beloved:
    fidelity is this, no more.
Be selfless in His district:
    purity is no more than this.

To become His intimate,
    render yourself selfless,
cast away "I" and "we":[1]
    fana is no more than this.

Be courageous in annihilation
    and forget this effacement;
if *fana* is forgotten,
    baqa is no more than this.

As long as you are conscious of self in your remembrance of God,
    you are heedless of God.
Seek silence:
    the gnosis of God is no more than this.

Be content with the will of the Friend
    and surrender to fate:
the path and the custom
    of sincere lovers is no more than this.

Passion, yearning, craving and rapture
    are limitations and signs of imperfection.
The perfected one is annihilated:
    our aim is no more than this.

O Nurbakhsh, in the creed of the *rendan*
    there is no discourse,
but if you must speak, what's been said here
    is sufficient — but no more than this!

ASK

Ask about my state when you have
    set aside "I" and "we."[1]
Come without self, then ask
    about the state of a selfless friend.

Go with sincerity
    to the lovers' tavern of ruin,
then ask the master
    about the mystery of *fana* and *baqa*.

Give away your own existence
    on the path to the Beloved,
then in the district of nothingness ask
    about fidelity and purity.

Let go of your desires, surrender to God's command
    without seeing yourself,
then ask
    about contentment.

Without the pain of love, don't go searching
    for remedies;
ask about medicine when you become afflicted
    with pain for Him.

Whatever problem you encounter
    on the path of love,
seek in yourself
    its cause and significance.

Turn your back on learned lectures
    about this world and the hereafter,
then go before the bestower of light and ask
    for discourses about God.

DON'T ASK

Don't ask us about anything
    but the affairs of love and fidelity;
don't ask us about the ascetic
    and his traditions of fear and hope.

Come drunkenly, without your self,
    come with purity and sincerity;
don't question us about wit and cleverness,
    or ask *why* and *how*.

In the banquet of the people of spiritual states
    leave chatter behind;
don't ask us about what is and what is not,
    or about what will be given or withheld.

Seek from us the path of *fana*,
    and the way to nothingness;
don't ask us about the affairs of the muftis[1]
    or the hypocritical mullahs.

In the *khaniqah*
    don't speak about yourself;
don't ask about wrath or mercy,
    or the calamities on heaven and earth.

At that gathering where wine drinkers
    are drunk and joyful,
leave behind your sense and reason;
    don't ask what is going on.

While with Nurbakhsh,
    don't even mention the memory of transient things.
Seek Unity;
    don't ask about anything other than God!

DON'T ASK *HOW* AND *WHY*

As long as you are still aware of yourself,
    don't ask of my state;
don't ask about the mystery of love
    and the nature of this affair.

As long as your petty intellect
    rules you,
don't ask about the place
    where love commands.

When you walk with sincerity
    towards the lane of the Friend,
submit to instruction and don't ask
    how and *why*.

Why do you try to trudge with your own feet
    on the path to Reality?
Beware! As long as you're a prisoner of self,
    don't ask about God.

This path cannot be traversed
    with the motives of vain desire;
with this still in your mind, don't ask about
    the path and conduct of the friends of God.

Our feast of madness does not admit
    rational people;
leave, keep away, and don't ask about
    where the mad ones drink.

Once Nurbakhsh lost consciousness
    of self,
he said, "Don't ask me about
    the realm of 'I' and 'you.'"[1]

THE CALL OF LOVE

In this lodge of existence
    we are but beggars of love,
servants of the world
    and humanity — for love.

Our own feet can no longer carry us;
    we traverse the path to union with God
only with His help and on
    the feet of love.

We saw no purity
    in the people of this age;
with heart and soul
    we adapted to the purity of love.

Only with the feet of tracelessness
    and the state of selflessness
may we reach
    the divine sanctuary of love.

On the ark of hope we are caught
    in the maelstrom of bewilderment —
our only hope is to be saved
    by the captain of love.

Don't ask us
    about belief or unbelief;
on our path, unbelief is everything
    other than love.

My heart is deeply saddened
    by the impudent intellect's realm;
O fortune, grant aspiration
    so that I may fly in the sky of love.

In the house of "I" and "you,"[1]
    there is nothing but headaches;
one must take refuge
    in the castle of love.

O Nurbakhsh, plug your ears
    so that with the heart's ear
you may hear
    the call of love.

THE LORD OF THE HEART

Once I cast off my existence
    for the heart,
I became a stranger to the self
    but acquainted with the heart.

Although the Kaaba in Mecca is the point of focus
    for a whole world,
I focus only on the Kaaba
    of the retreat of the heart.

I saw that the heart
    is His divine sanctuary;
I have cast out all other than the Friend
    from the space of the heart.

That which beats within the breast
    is not the heart.
The heart is the sublime throne,
    the seat of the Lord of the heart.

On the heart's path,
    the lovers become drowned in their blood;
many a destitute soul has been sacrificed
    at the threshold of the heart.

You are caught in the trap of lust
    and therefore know nothing of the heart;
you won't find the phoenix of the heart
    in the sky of the carnal soul.

Since Nurbakhsh departed from the domain
    of "I" and "you,"[1]
he has been resting contentedly
    in the sublime sanctuary of the heart.

THE HEART

Once I cast off my existence
  at the feet of the heart,
I became a stranger to the self
  but acquainted with the heart.

Everyone faces some direction to pray:
  mine is love,
and its sanctuary is the ambience
  of the heart.

Now that I've emptied
  the heart's chamber,
may the Beloved
  step inside.

The heart is not that organ
  in your chest;
it is the most sublime throne,
  where God is found.

In the cage of the body, no one ever witnessed
  the bird of the soul.
In the prison of the spirit, one cannot find
  the phoenix of the heart.

Many have been sacrificed
  on this path.
Many a lover's soul has been sacrificed
  for the heart's sake.

Since Nurbakhsh departed from the domain
  of "I" and "you,"[1]
he has been resting contentedly
  in the sublime sanctuary of the heart.

THE TAVERN'S THRESHOLD

I have settled down
    at the tavern's threshold;
I have settled down
    away from the people of the world.

Always dead drunk
    from remembering the Friend,
I have settled down,
    free from all chatter and commotion.

For a while I wandered from place to place,
    guided by the heart in search of Her;
now for Her sake, I have abandoned all movement
    and settled down.

The heart was trapped
    in the lasso of Her two tresses;
I have settled down
    in Her bewitching forelock's curl.

Those drunken eyes
    have robbed me of rest;
crazed, I have settled down
    in the curls of Her tresses.

Like a moth, my existence was burned away
    by the candle flame of Her face;
I am now ash and have settled down
    in her lush hair.

My Beloved
    asked about Nurbakhsh —
I said, "It is for Your sake that
    I have settled down without him."

THE SILENCE OF SOLITUDE

I have left behind my friends and homeland
    and have chosen
the dark night
    as my intimate companion.

Through remembering the Friend,
    I abandoned the restless crowd;
I am tranquil now, at rest
    in the lap of silence.

I am a stranger to acquaintances
    and no longer conscious of myself;
I spin in orbit
    on the other side of the cosmos.

Like Moses, I am lost
    in the valley of *fana*,
searching in bewilderment
    for the flames of a fire.

Like one who has been left behind
    by the caravan,
I look everywhere
    for the dust cloud left by a rider.

I was an image on water,
    then the wave of *fana* surged;
I have taken to my heels,
    running from the ocean.

I have lost Nurbakhsh,
    yet I do not seek news of him
so no one can tell me
    that I am in pursuit of something.

MANSURIAN WINE[1]

Since the day I made a pact
    of love with You,
I have been joyful, having given my heart
    to a crafty, drunken Turk.[2]

Your sun-like face
    has turned my breast into a fire-temple,
since I have given my heart
    to a fire-worshiper.

To conquer the land of the heart
    with the sword of love,
I have defeated on every front
    the army of "I" and "we."[3]

Every moment my Beloved travels
    from pre- to post-eternity.
Indeed I have thrown my heart at the feet
    of a swift heart-ravisher.

In the battle of love,
    I detached my heart from the world;
I have given Him the trophy
    of my own obliteration.

So that my Mansurian wine
    may render a whole world drunk,
I let my heart swim in blood
    and gave my body to the noose of the gallows.[4]

I am the bestower of light,
    freed from concern for my own being or non-being,
since I gave up my own existence
    for the love of the True Being.

THE FOLLOWERS OF LOVE

In this age I have found no refuge
    except in love;
I have seen no king
    but the master of the tavern.

Though there are armies
    in every nation,
I have seen no warriors
    like those who follow love.

Numerous kings have reigned
    in every era,
yet I have seen none that compares in stature
    to the king of love.

Monarchs wear golden crowns
    upon their heads,
but I have seen no finer adornment
    than the cap of *faqr*.

Though there are countless paths
    to the district of the Friend,
I have seen none
    more joyful than the tavern's path.

He will obliterate all else
    with just one glance.
Yes, I have seen no look
    like the gaze of the Friend.

I have seen resplendent beauties
    in every land;
O Light Bestower to the heart,
    I have never seen one as radiant as You!

ARGUMENTS

Last night, in frenzied madness
    and in the mood for arguments,
I had a confrontation
    with my turbulent heart.

"What did you choose in the end,
    belief or unbelief?" I asked.
"As long as I still had a choice,
    I was negligent of God," it replied.

"Are you a stranger or a friend —
    what is your state?" I asked.
"As long as I was a stranger
    I had a friend," it replied.

"Will you not speak of your union
    and separation?" I asked.
"I have repented,
    those thoughts were crude and simple!" it replied.

"Were you given sustenance
    by the Friend?" I asked.
"As long as I hoped for sustenance
    I remained destitute," it replied.

"Was the way to the district
    of that Sweetheart very far?" I asked.
"There was a path only
    as long as I had feet," it replied.

"Did you learn the mysteries
    of body and soul?" I asked.
"When did I ever pay attention
    to this body and soul?" it replied.

"When you were annihilated,
	what did your eyes behold?" I asked.
"I saw that my consciousness of self
	was baseless," it replied.

"Did the cloud of His Benevolence pour down
	the rain of His Mercy upon you?" I asked.
"When did I ever think of heaven
	and earth?" it replied.

"Are you freed
	from idol-worship?" I asked.
"As long as I still had any desire,
	I was worshiping an idol," it replied.

"Did your house prosper
	through the grace of His presence?" I asked.
"Every building I had
	was demolished by His hand!" it replied.

"Tell me this: were you satisfied
	with Nurbakhsh at last?" I asked.
"For no reason at all, I was caught up
	in arguments with him," it replied.

REMEMBERING YOU

In remembering You,
    I gave up both worlds;
for your sake,
    I gave up all "I" and "we."[1]

When my heart became detached
    from everything but You,
in drunkenness
    I gave up existence entirely.

Since You compassionately
    called me to Your district,
I gave up
    every wish and desire.

When the image of Your face
    appeared from every side,
I gave up
    all spiritual states and stations.

I found You to be the peace
    of my impassioned soul;
then I gave up
    all sorrow, pain and cure.

When I surrendered my head
    on your path,
I embraced Your affirmation
    and gave up negation.[2]

Nurbakhsh wants You
    for Yourself.
Therefore, he says,
    "I gave up this world and the hereafter."

THE INTERPRETED SIGN

You ask me why, in my youth,
    I became old?
I saw the stunning stature of that beauty
    and was struck still.

Good news, O men of reason:
    madness has passed all bounds!
Again I began a journey within myself
    and was chained like a madman.

When I saw the destinies
    of the world's empires
I gave up my scheming
    and followed fate.

What joy to be paralyzed by You!
    You already know
it was Your charming spell
    that conquered me.

The worldly dream, not needing interpretation,
    left my mind;
I became freed from
    wanting explanations.

You are the same now
    as You were in the beginning,
yet I am the sign[1]
    whose interpretation is worthy of You.

Nurbakhsh, what sin is this
    that you speak of yourself?
I am not to blame
    if I seem to transgress.

THE SILENT LOVER

Good news, friends! I am freed
    from the bonds of "I" and "we";[1]
in His inner chambers
    I became privy to every secret.

I have forgotten the fables
    in the book of reason;
I am a love story,
    and I originated from love.

My head was filled with desire
    for the crown of madness,
so I joined the lovers who have lost their hearts
    and gambled away my life.

To hear graceful words
    from that blossom-like mouth,
I kept company
    with the beggars at His door.

O Beloved, I am the same silent lover,
    separated from You —
it is only for You and through Your expression
    that I have become so eloquent.

I have no interest in
    the art of poetry —
it is only out of desire for You that I have spent
    a lifetime composing such rhymes.

Through the Beloved's breath
    Nurbakhsh was singing drunkenly:
"Your words have been flowing from my mouth
    ever since I became intimate with You."

PASSION FOR MADNESS

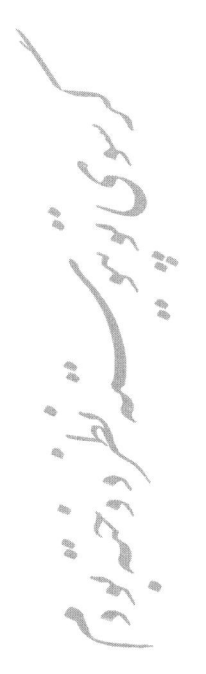

If I have fixed my gaze constantly
    in Your direction,
it was because of the passion for madness
    that I had learnt.

In the face of Your flirtatious rejections
    I, a needy dervish,
made You a gift of my entire savings:
    my heart and my soul.

A moth found me transfixed
    by Your candle's flame;
the poor creature knew not
    that I had burnt away.

All my life I kept the candle of the intellect
    alight on Your path.
As soon as love arrived
    it was snuffed out,

And the patched cloak of union with You
    that I had stitched together
with passion's needle
    was torn into a hundred pieces.

You pardoned Nurbakhsh[1]
    and chose him[2]
long before he sold himself
    to You.

THE FABLE OF EXISTENCE

For a lifetime I ran anxiously
>   in every direction,
then I flashed like lightning
>   from the glance of Your eyes.

Bewildered,
>   I clung to Your hair,
but I saw no hope;
>   there were only dark days for me.

You did not say, "Look, here lies one
>   vanquished by Me."
You did not even look at me
>   or give me hope.

You sold me for nothing,
>   O You, Essence of Being;
I gave my self up
>   to attain You.

Have You forgotten me?
>   I do not believe it,
for in despair
>   You are my only hope.

I heard these words
>   from Nurbakhsh,
which he sang
>   as he was walking by:

"I am happy that I surrendered
>   the fable of my self to the Friend
and became
>   remembered by Him."

THE HOPE OF ALL EXISTENCE

I am that poor beggar
    who comes to You with neediness.
I am weary of self-display;
    I will not even glance at being.

I, a destitute one —
    who am I to ask for anything?
To where should I turn my face,
    from whom should I hide?

O You, the hope of all existence,
    I am perplexed. Who is there besides You
to say to You, face to face,
    "Listen, I have a secret to tell"?

I, a drunkard, find myself here,
    where there is no beloved but You.
So to whom should I turn and say,
    "I desire to pray"?

By the truth of the Truth,
    You are both truth and illusion.
Yet my heart did not hear me when I said,
    "I am aware of illusion."

With a song You stole my heart and soul,
    my belief and unbelief.
I have now forgotten my companions
    and can no longer tolerate the melodies of the lute.

Now, what can the impoverished Nurbakhsh
    seek or desire?
To which Kaaba can he turn and say,
    "I wish to make a pilgrimage"?

THE SIGN OF TRACELESSNESS

I swear that as long as I am alive
    I shall not feel offended by You;
I shall walk to Your district
    and place my head on Your doorstep.

My hope of union with You
    was a vain fancy.
How can a temporal being reach the Eternal?
    How could I ever think this?

I shall not lament my separation from You
    because You are completely faithful;
it is because of my heart and eyes
    that I moan and cry.

Through Your eyes I search for
    an image of Your face —
this is the sole token
    of my tracelessness.

I have heard that You remember me
    every moment
because I have kept the memory of Your face
    in the core of my soul.

Through yearning, I became freed
    from the memory of self.
How then could the house of my heart
    preserve the memory of other things?

Since Nurbakhsh has no opportunity
    to speak,
I will recount his state
    on his behalf.

TRANSFIXED BY THE CUPBEARER'S FACE

With languishing eyes
    I am so transfixed by the Cupbearer's face
that I no longer care for Her goblet
    or the wine inside.

I am that shattered cup,
    so drunk from Her beauty
that I am not interested in the chalice,
    and I won't lose my calm.

I desire neither union nor separation;
    I care not for pain or cure.
All volition has slipped away
    from the control of my free will.

Why ask me about belief and unbelief
    when I am beyond both?
Why ask me of my state
    when I have left my self?

I won't set out for the garden,
    for I can't tell rose from thorn.
My expectant eyes
    have turned away from both worlds.

I am freed from identity and name
    and have left behind all customs.
I am no longer involved
    with the people of the world.

If from the realm of Unity
    with the tongue of the people of multiplicity
Nurbakhsh has spoken vain words
    I am utterly ashamed.

DESIRE FOR YOU

Tonight I am crazy, crazy
    with desire for You.
This impassioned heart of mine
    is fervently longing for You.

My strength and endurance
    have both run out;
now I am waiting, with expectant eyes,
    for sublime aspiration from You.

Your face
    is turned towards others
as if unaware that my gaze
    is fixed upon Your lovely stature.

You wander about drunkenly,
    disregarding me,
as if unaware
    that all I care about is You.

O potency of every wine,
    O motivator of every yearning!
My soul-inflaming intoxication
    comes from Your blood-red wine.

O Spirit, O You with the breath of Christ,[1]
    O object of man's adoration!
My heart lies crucified
    in Your curls.[2]

Night has departed, dawn is here,
    and I am drunk, while You lie languishing;
yet still this impassioned head of mine
    has fixed its eyes on Your azure goblet.

Due to separation from You, O source of all desire,
    I have melted away,
heading towards Your ocean
    afloat on the flood of my tears.

Out of friendship and generosity,
    forgive Nurbakhsh,
for tonight I am crazy, crazy
    with desire for You.

LONGING FOR YOU

O Beloved, You are my helper;
    I fly towards You
and tear this bodily garment
    from my soul.

There is no profit
    in "I" and "you";[1]
it is best to leave it all
    behind.

Let me sit and surrender my head
    at Your feet;
let me rise and deliver my soul
    to Your hands.

Let me foster the longing for You
    in my head,
wipe all but consciousness of You
    from my heart.

Let me borrow another eye
    from You
and see Your visage
    with Your eye.

Every place I pass by
    I see You present;
I'm a nobody, head over heels
    in love with You.

I am ready to be sacrificed
    to Your countenance,
for I have lost all news
    of myself.

When You bestow light upon me,
    I shall fly
with Your wings, in Your abode,
    with no self.

A LOST HEART

How can I retrieve my heart
 from Him? It is lost to me.
And I no longer have the head that might call for
 another round of love.

Where should I go? Whom should I ask?
 Whom should I go on seeking?
I have reached the point where
 I don't want to be conscious of myself.

My eyes behold Your face
 with Your light.
How could I possibly see
 anything other than You?

I shall not speak about anything
 but love;
I shall turn a deaf ear to every word
 that is not about You.

The holy sanctuary sought by all
 is manifest inside me.
Why then should I set out on a journey
 to the Kaaba?

To behold Your face,
 I became void of self;
I had to accomplish this
 without wasting a moment.

You bestowed light to my soul
 through Your sun-like face;
You did not want me
 to keep turning toward the moon.

ALAS

Who am I? A homeless vagrant,
    a nobody, a lover
freed from any "I" and "you"[1] spoken by
    the people of desire.

My heart has shrunk away from
    these shallow hypocrites
who pretend to be unruffled.
    I am a lover of the realness of riffraff.

Any animal has more honor
    than these people.
The companionship of animals is sufficient
    for me in this world.

It is only through deception that human beings are called
    superior to all other creatures.
True humanity only exists
    in the books around me.

All are busy fulfilling
    the ego's desire.
What can I say?
    I am in prison in my own home.

Alas, Nurbakhsh, everywhere
    you're saying:
there is no beautiful one in this town
    to be remembered by.

TRANSFIXED BY IDOLS

You have become a selfless
    enraptured lover — I know,
You have become totally helpless
    on my path — I know.

Desiring madness you have relinquished
    religion, heart and reason;
it is not for nothing
    that you are disgraced — I know.

Since you left your self
    in the tavern,
you have become free
    from the shackles of desire — I know.

When you built an idol-temple
    in the Kaaba of the heart,
you became transfixed
    by idols — I know.

I have news from you
    that you have no news of your self;
you have become free
    from the need for news — I know.

"I" and "we"[1] is the source
    of all agitation and misfortune;
you have become free
    from self — I know.

Nurbakhsh, this poem
    is not based on erudite style.
Yes, you have become freed
    from the chains of the intellect — I know.

THE SIN OF SELF-ASSERTION

Let me declare it outright:
    I am ashamed of myself
and my being — such has the hand of fate
    molded my clay.

Who am I? A helpless one,
    unaware of either head or foot.
Day and night my soul is ablaze
    with the fire of love.

I am a dust-mote, dancing in the air of…
    I will say no more.
A dust-mote, I said — no, much less!
    I am ashamed of what I said.

Out of desire for Him I burn
    like a candle,
but I am disgusted
    with my own flame's self-display.

Self-assertion is a sin
    that the Friend does not forgive;
with a single glance,
    He cut me off from "I" and "we."[1]

Thirty years have passed for me,
    though it seems many more;
I am now unaware
    of the passing years.

I am Nurbakhsh….No, who am I? Nothing.
    What was I? A shadow.
What did I become? Effaced. For whom?
    For the One who brings peace to my heart.

THE WORLD AND THE SPIRITUAL REALM

I am my own veil
    and the goal of my heart.
I bring all this pain
    and suffering on myself.

Who am I? I am naught,
    no need to ponder.
There is only one Being, and He
    is expressing this point through my mouth.

Let me tell you openly,
    I have no mouth;
He is my eyes, my ears,
    and all my limbs.

Forget Greek philosophy and the mysteries
    of the spiritual realm;
in truth, He, not I, is all there has ever been
    and all that really exists.

Who am I? A fancy, a dream,
    an image on water.
It is only through habit
    that you see me in my body.

He is unveiled and manifest
    in every marketplace;
but I, an impassioned one,
    have become an enduring fable.

The Truth is the bestower of light
    to everyone, everywhere.
It is not my fault
    if you have not comprehended my words.

DISCOURSE ON THOUGHTS

I decided to give up my soul
    for His sake.
"That is for Me to decide;
    I will take it if I wish!" He responded.

"Don't start a discourse on your thoughts
    and opinions!" He said.
"Certainly. I shall do
    whatever You wish!" I responded.

"Renounce everything
    in the name of love!" He said.
"I pledge my life and soul
    to Your eyes!" I responded.

"Who are you
    to walk towards Me?" He said.
"It is always with Your feet
    that I move across space," I responded.

"Why have you erased
    all trace of your self?" He asked.
"To aim for the vicinity
    of Your lane," I responded.

"Keeping the secrets
    is the rule of the path," He said.
"Other than You
    I have nothing to hide," I responded.

"Tell me,
    what news of Nurbakhsh?" He asked.
"I know nothing of him
    to tell," I responded.

CLAIMING TO LOVE

Who am I to assert myself
	before You,
or to talk to anyone
	of my love for You?

I am that zero
	that is counted as naught;
considerations of inner journey and outer conduct
	no longer apply.

I am too lowly
	to even make known that I am naught;
don't ask me to observe the secret
	and prevent its revelation.

From pre- to post-eternity
	there is clearly one Being alone;
if I talk about body and soul,
	it is all just a fiction.

I have seen plainly
	that He is both the idol and the idol-worshiper.
So why should I speak
	of the idol-breaker?

O mullah, I cannot discern belief from unbelief!
	Be silent,
or I might divulge your secret
	in public.

I have had no news of Nurbakhsh
	for many years,
and have forgotten
	how to be conscious of self.

THE REED PIPE AND THE PLAYER

He who has been searching for You
    an entire lifetime — is me.
He who has been enraptured
    by Your face — is me.

He who looks with favor on everyone
    in every place — is You.
He whose eyes have been fixed on You
    everywhere — is me.

He who torments
    the faithful ones — is You.
He who has loved
    this habit of Yours — is me.

He who has ravished our hearts
    with disheveled curls — is You.
He whose heart
    has been bound to Your braid — is me.

He who displays
    a braid of hair like a polo bat is You.
He who has been a rolling ball
    at Your feet — is me.[1]

He who has captured all
    in the impasse[2] of bewilderment — is You.
He who has been transfixed
    by Your beautiful face[3] — is me.

Nurbakhsh is the reed pipe;
    his player — is You.
He who has always been
    Your spokesman — is me.

THE MIRACLE OF NON-BEING

I am the interpreter of loving-kindness;
    I am the guide of love.
For the souls of the lovers of God
    I am the burning coal and the raging fire.

I am the guide of the travelers seeking Unity
    on the feet of aspiration;
I am the wings of the birds
    in the sky of love.

A loving guardian of the sanctuary
    of peace and purity,
I am the door and threshold
    of the house of sincerity and fidelity.

I am the cupbearer for the companions
    in the tavern of ruin;
I am the fervor in the hearts
    of all people, whether believers or not.

The Sufi's only miracle is non-being;
    Who am I?
I am the clear sign and demonstration
    of non-existence.

When intoxicated and no longer conscious of self
    I am the ruler of existence;
when I return to myself
    I am less than worthless.

I speak with the tongue of the Beloved,
    unaware of self;
I am the light bestower to mankind and the world,
    the barren and verdant alike.

I AM NOT ME

You are my inward dimension and my outward aspect.
    I am not me. I am without I.
You are my absence and my presence.
    I am not me. I am without I.

Creation is but appearance; You are True Being.
    I am non-existent; You are existence.
You are the essence of my appearances.
    I am not me. I am without I.

To me You are the shadow and radiance.
    To me You are the rose and the garden.
To me You are both the viewer and the viewed.
    I am not me. I am without I.

Non-being gained existence through You.
    An entire world became drunk through You.
You are my wine and pitcher.
    I am not me. I am without I.

You are my wrath and my affection.
    You are my darkness and my light.
To me You are the unbeliever as well as the believer.
    I am not me. I am without I.

In my head resides desire for You.
    My heart's retreat is Your dwelling.
You are my observer and my concealer.
    I am not me. I am without I.

O You Who brings joy to me,
    my sun[1] and light bestower,
You are my clear sign:
    I am not me. I am without I.

HIS SPLENDOR

How can I express
    what I see in this veil?
There is only one Being,
    but I see a myriad of "I's" and "we's."[1]

I observe the light of existence
    to come from His splendor.
I see all the "we's" and "you's"[2] to be
    only imaginary forms.

Being the slave of love
    is my only occupation.
I see everyone as a beggar
    in the presence of that King.

I am unimpressed
    by this world and the next;
I see both these abodes
    as desolate appearances.

The world is alive through Him,
    while He lives through Himself alone.
I see creation as a caravan
    traveling to *fana*.

His sun-like visage
    removed the shadow of multiplicity;
I see His luminous face
    everywhere.

Nurbakhsh,
    why all these cryptic expressions?
Divulge the secret:
    I see God by God![3]

SECRETS OF LOVE

Gone is the time of separation,
    sorrow, pain and pining;
the heart-illuminating firmament
    turns to the heart's desire.

We are happy and dead drunk
    in the Friend's quarters;
We sip wine dregs at night
    and clear wine by day.

I say, "If You shall torment me yet again,
    tell me now!"
He answers, "More blame and hardship
    will come your way."

If not for the Beloved's grace,
    flowing tears and
heart-scorching sighs would have borne
    no results.

I was so utterly steeped
    in ecstasy and spiritual states
that to me both mid-summer and autumn
    seemed like springtime.

I praise the high honor
    of the tavern of ruin,
where, out of reverence, even the king kisses
    the threshold of that mender of rags.

Nurbakhsh, be silent.
    Why reveal the secrets of love?
Where there is love
    no secret remains.

THE EPIPHANY OF YOUR BEAUTY

For an entire lifetime
    I have been continuously absorbed by You,
adapting to the good and the evil
    of the people of this world, for Your sake.

The epiphany of Your beauty
    has never changed,
and I, too, am the same lover
    who lost his heart to You.

I am but the dust
    that settles in Your quarters;
I am the wax
    that has melted in Your hand.

In Your district I sought refuge
    from attention to anything other than You;
I flew away from myself
    towards You.

I have closed my heart's eyes
    to both worlds
ever since I first looked
    upon Your lovely face.

It has been said we must know ourselves
    to know You —
I have known no one
    other than You.

You have been occupied much
    with Nurbakhsh,
and I, too, have been absorbed by You
    for an entire lifetime.

THE LAND OF "WE" AND "YOU"[1]

I have left
    the land of "we" and "you."
Now I sit waiting
    for a side-long glance from Him.

I have uttered nothing in my whole life
    apart from the talk of love.
Never have I hurt the feelings
    of even an ant in anger.

Having gone through the annals
    of time and space,
I feel bored with acquaintances
    and weary of strangers.

I have shredded the scrolls
    of leadership and guidance,
and shattered the mirror
    of discipleship and masterhood.

Inform all idolaters
    of my state;
I have become free from the idol of me
    formed by your imagination.

I have erased the traces of phenomena
    from the tablet of my soul,
and untied the attachments to everything
    except God from my heart.

Not only have I cut the bond
    of masterhood and leadership,
I have also leapt out of the trap
    of existence altogether.

He has been my bestower of light
    everywhere,
ever since I left
    the land of "we" and "you."

THE PASSION OF LOVING

I have pawned my Sufi cloak
> at the tavern.
I gave up my heart
> to my beloved.

Don't ask me why there is "much of this"
> and "little of that" in this world;
however little or much I had
> I gave up on the Friend's path.

Don't ask me to answer
> the arguments of reason;
I left this debate
> to the sober folk.

In the district of love
> there remains neither faith nor unbelief;
I left this bait and trap
> to the customers who deal in such wares.

The passion of loving
> expelled "I" and "we";[1]
in this affair,
> I gave up all I possessed or could possess.

You ask me who I am? Nothing.
> What do I want? Nothing.
I have left my fate
> in the Beloved's hands.

Last night, with Nurbakhsh,
> I drank from love's cup,
then pawned him too
> at the tavern.

LOVE'S MADNESS

O minstrel, we have fallen
    far beyond the reach of reason tonight;
we are game if you play
    the tune of madness until dawn.

Our song of Unity is composed of
    longing sighs and the heart's wailing;
we have left behind our selves,
    rosary and prayer rug.

We are not interested in profiting from
    the wares of faith and unbelief;
on the path of love and affection,
    we handed over the cash of our self-existence.

If you have heard that we are *rendan*
    it is true;
but if you are simple,
    we will be simple with you.

We have felt the agitation of a fervent love
    in the vat of the heart;
we are now more intoxicating
    than a hundred jugs of wine.

O Nurbakhsh, there is no freedom
    from the chains of love's madness;
having escaped the bounds of "I" and "we,"[1]
    we are free.

THE PATH OF LOVE

I've spent my entire life worn out
    on the path of Your love;
I have laid my head on the threshold
    of Your tavern.

I've sat awaiting a glance
    from You;
I languish, craving a mouthful
    from the wine cup.

I am not afraid to deal with Your flirtatious glance,
    but I have lost all my neediness.
I've thrown my being to the winds
    in the lane of Your love.

If the man of reason mocks,
    he is unaware
that we live through love, having been born
    through Your love.

O Royal Rider, do not turn Your face
    away from me;
Without a knight or a queen,
    I'm just a beggar pawn.

Every moment You play
    a thousand different roles;
have mercy on me,
    as I am just a simpleton.

Look upon Nurbakhsh
    with mercy —
but for Your own pleasure,
    since I am bereft of choice.

WARES OF NON-EXISTENCE

Since we took reign
    in the realm of loving,
we have built anew
    the edifice of love.

In love's marketplace, we gave up
    our imaginary existence
and for a lifetime have been trading
    in the wares of non-existence.

To become an intimate
    in the Beloved's sanctuary,
we purified our heart from the thought
    of anything other than Him.

We have been free for years
    from the bonds of creation;
don't imagine that
    we have just now left captivity.

It is through logical argument
    that the philosopher affirms God.
We, however, have pointed the way to Him
    through self-negation.

From the very first day,
    we have erased with the hand of love
the words "sorrow," "toil" and "bitterness"
    from the tablet of the heart.

The mystics say
    our eye is the bestower of light
since we have looked upon ourselves
    with scornful eyes.

THE SEEKERS OF GOD

We seekers of God
    are strangers in your world.
You may have wisdom,
    as for us — we are all mad.

We are not like the candle
    that weeps at the touch of any flame.
We are ablaze from head to toe,
    but laughing like *rendan* — that is what we are.

Our wings and plumes were scorched
    repeatedly by the Friend's candle flame.
Yet we stood our ground —
    we are not like that moth.

When the spell of "I" and "we"[1] was broken
    with the rock of madness,
we realized clearly
    that we are both treasure and ruin.

We lost our self-worship
    in the district of idol-worship.
Stop reproaching us, O mullah,
    for living in the idol-temple!

Have you so forgotten the enormity of the covenant
    that you brought the measuring cup?[2]
Don't you realize that we determine
    the portions?

O Nurbakhsh, the Cupbearer of the pre-eternal banquet
    pours wine according to each one's capacity,
until His dregs transform us
    into precious pearls.

THE BEGGARS OF THE TAVERN OF RUIN

We, beggars
   in the tavern of ruin,
drink the wine
   of His pure essence.

Selfless from
   the colorless wine,
we are the mirror image
   of God's countenance.

We played the backgammon of love with Him,
   and the Beloved won.
In chess we were checkmated
   by the Friend's rook.[1]

We do not belong
   to the people of prayer and litany;
we have stopped
   petitioning God.

In every direction
   we see the face of the Beloved,
not seeking the Kaaba
   or other holy places.

We are annihilated from self
   and free from others;
we are far away from the mullah
   and his hypocritical nonsense.

We are the bestower of light
   and the enemy of the pretentious;
we annul the magic and miracles
   of false pretenders.

LOVE'S TREASURE

Don't ask me anything,
    for I am no sage.
Do not veil your face from me,
    for I am no stranger.

My heart is bleeding,
    but I am not tearful like the candle;
unlike the moth,
    I keep my burning hidden inside.

That pundit of the city
    who praised me for my knowledge
was crazy to say
    I am not mad.

The cupbearer
    sent me to the vat-house
after hearing I was not content
    with cup, bowl or jar.

I have fallen into the vat,
    happy and drunk;
there is nothing left of me now
    but what the wine seller serves in the tavern.

I found lover, beloved and their love story
    to be nothing but tales —
I am rid of them now;
    I don't pursue fables.

Love is a treasure,
    lover and beloved the spell;
I don't roam the ruins
    hunting for buried gold.[1]

Why, you ask, did Nurbakhsh
    give his heart to love?
I said at the beginning:
    I am no sage.

THE WORK OF LOVING

I've had no beloved
    since pre-eternity except You;
I've been involved with no one
    other than You.

You've always been occupied
    with others;
I've found no peace
    with anyone but You.

I found tranquility
    in the lasso of Your tress;
I've had neither the thought
    nor the ability to flee.

The motion of all existence
    is in Your hands;
I've had no orbit or motion
    without You.

You are Your own lover;
    there is no other being but You.
I who have lost my heart to You
    have no friend or homeland.

Your being is the bright day
    hidden from my eyes;
without Your face
    I have seen only dark nights.

O Light Bestower of the soul,
    in this music-making universe,
my lot has been mournful sighs
    with every breath.

CRAVING FOR DESIRE[1]

I found in my heart
    the treasure of divine names;
no one knows
    about what I found.

My heart slipped out of my control
    through remembrance of His face.
I found a haven
    in the sanctuary of love.

I became enraptured and exposed
    through His love;
then I found that He, too,
    was unveiled.

I forgot about His promise
    of "tomorrow"
when I found His paradise
    in this world.

I abandoned the craving
    for desire[2]
when I found desire
    to be His veil.

For union with Him
    I surrendered my head.
On the path I found
    an agile step.

Nurbakhsh became
    so drunk on wine
that I found him unique and exceptional
    in the realm of drunkenness.

THE PALACE OF LOVING-KINDNESS

As soon as we entered the realm
    of loving-kindness and compassion,
we trampled the stuff of impermanence
    and pre-eternity, too.

We washed away the image of other things
    from the mind
until we spoke of our fidelity
    before the Beloved.

Sincerely, we tore away the veils
    of identity and fame
and out of love pitched our tent
    beyond existence and non-being.

The gold of the realm of possibilities
    increased in value
when we minted the coins
    of purity and love.

Ecstatically, we demolished
    the edifice of selfhood
and with the hands of yearning built
    the palace of loving-kindness.

We ignored the distinctions
    of custom and religion;
in love, we banished thoughts of quantity and quality
    from the kingdom of the heart.

By remembrance of the Friend, we were saved
    from the plight of multiplicity;
from the ocean of "no god," we arrived
    to raise a banner on the shore of "but God."[1]

The *khaniqah* of compassion and fidelity
    is no place for debate;
we erased from the book
    all that was not about the Friend.

We walked the land of loving-kindness
    and compassion,
where His sun-like face
    bestowed light to the soul.

BEAUTY'S CUSTOMER

Though I became a customer
    of Your beauty,
It was You who made me yearn
    to meet You in the first place.

When I saw Your seditious
    and narcissus-resembling eyes,
I became afflicted
    and kept company with pain.

I lost my self-existence
    in Your district;
I surrendered my heart
    and followed my beloved.

I surrendered myself joyfully
    to both Your kindness and Your wrath
ever since you extracted
    the confession[1] from us.

Who am I
    to negate myself?
Your manifestation
    caused that negation.

Spiritual wayfaring and social conduct,
    wayfarer and path,
are all illusions; I feel destitute
    and weary of them all.

Pre- to post-eternity
    is but one breath;
Nurbakhsh was heard saying,
    "It is as if I never existed."

DRUNK FROM INTIMACY WITH YOU

Yearning for You has been lodged in my heart
    all my life;
my heart is attached
    to Your crucifix-like curls.

I washed my hands of everything
    to grasp the hem of Your dress;
I bound myself to You,
    for You are all I care about.

I shut my eyes to everything else
    in order to see You;
I rejected everything
    in desiring You.

I won't walk the path of the sober,
    as I am drunk;
in my lowliness
    I gaze up at Your lofty stature.

I did not listen to any words
    that concern something other than You;
I sat in silence,
    since your commotion is within me.

I cut myself off from myself
    and then reached Your quarter;
I passed beyond negation,
    since I have Your affirmation.

I won't complain
    if You won't bestow light;[1]
I am drunk from intimacy with you
    and enjoy Your friendship.

THE BEGGARS OF LOVE

I am a beggar at love's door,
    having left myself behind;
I am a stranger in the whole city,
    homeless everywhere.

O religious hypocrite, you can have His paradise
    and all the virgins therein.
I will not go anywhere; instead I will remain
    in the dust by His door.

I'll take drunkenness and madness;
    leave the mullah to his supplications and prayers.
How could he know my state,
    as I am unconscious of my self?

On the path of fidelity I cannot tell
    head from foot.
There is a world of difference between
    the petty mullah and me.

I've shut my self-seeing eyes
    in the tavern of the ruin;
I can now behold God's face clearly
    with His own eyes.

From His love I have attained
    an eagle-like splendor.
I will not fly away from His district of loving-kindness
    in search of worthless desires.

Nurbakhsh left behind everyone
    when he sat with the Friend,
saying, "I want only the Friend,
    as other than Him is worthless."

THE BELOVED

An entire lifetime we have remained captives
    in our own cage.
This much is clear: we cannot stay settled
    in this trap.

O Beloved, cast a glance our way;
    have mercy,
for we are the poor and destitute
    of Your lane.

O auspicious master, you who pay no
    attention to us,
through your love our hearts grow young,
    however old we may be.

Ever since your sun-like love brought light
    to the house of the heart
our minds have been at peace,
    far from both cleric and king.

Once we heard Gabriel's call
    at the tavern door,
we became strangers to the melodies and songs
    of the world.

Come back and take this self away,
    that only You might remain:
We've been weary and fed up with our own existence
    for such a long time.

We've washed our hands of everything
    that You might bestow light:
We've surrendered our heads on Your path
    and lie ready to die at Your feet.

THE WAVES OF THE OCEAN OF LOVE

For a lifetime, the intellect toyed with me
>   on the path to the Beloved,
trying to convince me that I was in love
>   with Your face.

But how can I even speak of Your sun-like love
>   when I am but a shadow
caressed by the dancing flame
>   of Your candle.

My imaginary existence was like the ripples
>   on the water's surface,
a pattern erased by waves
>   of the ocean of love.

I have taken refuge in God
>   from both reality and appearance
so that He might cure
>   my self-existence.

Once He saw that I have no need
>   for this world and the hereafter,
He ravished my heart and soul
>   with His coquettish spell.

On my journey towards Him,
>   I trampled upon both worlds:
on seeing me charge ahead fearlessly,
>   He finally took my hand.

How can I set out on the hajj
>   intending to see You
when the heart itself is my Kaaba,
>   not some stone in Arabia?

I have told you about Nurbakhsh
>   and the ups and downs of love's path
so you will know that God alone
>   has been the reason for my triumph.

THE LOVERS WHO GAMBLE LIFE AWAY

We are noble drunks, lovers ready
    to gamble our lives.
Everyone is proud of somebody;
    God is the pride of our lives.

If the Beloved wishes, we'll give up
    spirit, heart and soul,
and if He permits we'll throw our heads down
    at His feet.

The capital of Sufism is selflessness
    and contentment —
we have set our hearts on God and are in harmony
    with whatever He wills.

There's room within our chests
    only for love and purity;
in the workshop of existence we are confidants
    of this mystery.

Until pain and suffering for His sake become
    the cure of our hearts,
we will not become involved with anything
    but love's sorrow for Him.

We have donated the catch of both worlds
    to our Beloved.
We want no carcasses;
    we are falcons, not vultures.

At every moment God bestows light
    on our souls,
while we go racing passionately
    towards Him.

THE DEPARTED CARAVAN

We are tavern-dwellers
    controlled by our breath.
We are nobodies in the two worlds
    and are free from "I" and "we."[1]

Out of longing for Him, we were never involved
    with anyone but the Predator,
and so never noticed that all our lives
    we were stuck in a cage.

When we truly set foot
    in the kingdom of *fana*,
we became free from policeman,
    magistrate and judge.

Now the caravan has gone;
    drunk, we have lost the way.
We are unaware of self and
    the cries and bells of the caravan's departure.

We know neither heaven
    nor hell.
We are not disturbed by the passion and excitement
    of lustful people.

Through God we see God's light everywhere.
    We are not like Moses,
contemplating Sinai
    and a burning bush instead.

With You, O Friend, we are not ourselves —
    for it is from Your light
that we bestow light
    and are beyond the reach of others.

THE HOUSE OF SINCERITY AND PURITY

Come, and without thinking of "I" and "we"[1]
    we will free each other of sorrow;
without rest we will bring peace to each other
    and care for each other.

Through love, we will make fidelity
    and compassion our watchwords;
separated from harshness and harm,
    we will be with each other.

Without conditions or complaints,
    we will sacrifice ourselves for each other;
without obligation and pretention,
    we will be lovers of each other.

We will become strangers to everyone
    and view our selves as insignificant;
we will clear away the dust of sorrow
    and become friends of each other.

We will find our home
    in the house of sincerity and purity;
without thought of name or position
    we will honor each other.

We will fly with shared wings
    to a realm beyond both time and space;
in the sky of the Truth
    we will orbit each other.

We will pour wine from the vat of love
    and fill each other's goblet;
we will forever be the cupbearer
    and drunkard, languishing for each other.

Ah, how sweetly a loving friend
    said to Nurbakhsh:
"Come, and without thinking of 'I' and 'we'
    we will free each other of sorrow."

THE PEOPLE OF LOVING-KINDNESS

We are the people of loving-kindness,
    leaders and guides of one another;
through the purity of love
    we are helpers of one another.

Though in body separate, we are all
    but one spirit;
we are all the soul, spirit, heart and beloved
    of one another.

We are all one people:
    without "you" and "I" there is only "we,"
all equal, all love, all companions
    of one another.

No one but us is allowed
    to enter our private quarters.
We are all tied to each other, all sympathetic
    with one another.

Each one would sacrifice himself
    for the other here.
All are candles and moths, all flowers and gardens
    for one another.

Without doubt, our assembly is
    an intimate retreat.
All are selfless, drunk and sober
    from one another.

The armies of the self
    have fled from us,
for we are fellow soldiers here,
    all commanders of one another.

Our pain requires
    neither doctor nor remedy.
We are all the cure and the patient
    for one another.

If you call for someone here,
    all will answer, "Yes!"
for all have one name; all are companions,
    cohorts of one another.

Our place is the house of love,
    full of passion and music,
for all are songs, reed pipes and lutes
    for one another.

O Nurbakhsh, it is from being without
    "I" and "we"[1]
that we are the merchants and customers
    of one another.

ARISE!

Arise! Let's break up the foundation
    of "I" and "you"[1] and
with love's aid block all thoughts
    of "more" and "less" from the heart.

Let's leave the city
    of foul-natured people,
and reside in the district of the beautiful,
    to speak only of love.

There is no safety in the realm
    of "we" and "you";[2]
let's step out from multiplicity and
    enter into Unity.

Let's spend our time
    in joy
and not talk about sorrow,
    or cry and moan.

Let's become free from needing
    this world or the hereafter.
Let's cut down all idols
    with the blade of detachment.

Let's chase away the army of thought
    with the Friend's remembrance,
and block the army of grief
    by the Friend's grace.

With Nurbakhsh let's drink
    from the vat of Unity
and play the melodies of *shur* and *nava*[3]
    with the lute of love.

THE THRESHOLD OF LOVING-KINDNESS

With a glance I cure
    the pain of love
and, in the crucible of purity, turn
    the heart's copper to gold.

Faced with the Friend's coquettish rejection,
    I gave up everything to prove my neediness;
I abandoned all claims
    before the sanctuary of His fidelity.

I have gained admittance
    to the tavern of ruin,
so why should I make myself the prisoner
    of some egotistic mullah?

The melody of the divine covenant
    plays in my heart,
so why should I pay attention
    to the mullah's claims?

From the moment the master
    of the fire worshipers became my guide,
I have followed him faithfully
    in the ways and manners of love.

You have been stuck for a lifetime
    at the threshold of loving-kindness —
leave behind your self now and join us
    in pure friendship.

The angels led Nurbakhsh
    to the tavern, saying,
"It is to please God that we
    perform this service."

THE TRANSITORY "I" AND "WE"[1]

I'll abandon this transitory
    "I" and "we."
I'll clear away this make-believe existence
    of mine.

O giver of advice, don't frighten me
    with talk of the hazards of the path.
I'll be galloping along towards His district
    on His feet.

In the school of love and purity,
    the intellect has no authority.
I will not take heed of the books
    of Avicenna and Razi.

I view the creation as
    the Friend's newly-planted trees.
I will not discriminate among
    Turks, Arabs and Hindus.

Every creature has come to existence
    through the generosity of God's being.
I will express my compassion
    to whomever I see.

Day and night, before the coyness
    of the Mahmud of the Soul,
I express my love like Ayaz:[2]
    with the goods of nothingness.

Do not speak of union with Him —
    no being has the capacity to bear it.
O Nurbakhsh, in my heart I love God
    through remembrance of Him.

THE PROMISE OF SEEING HIM

Tonight, with love we're going
    to the door of the Friend;
in madness we're setting out
    in search of the Beloved.

Tonight, we'll leave behind
    the city of the self
and make our way to His lane
    on the promise of seeing Him.

Tonight, our jug is broken
    and our goblet lost;
unconscious of self we're going
    to the vintner's house.

Tonight, we'll rend our garments
    at the feast of love and madness;
away from people's eyes,
    we'll pursue the Beloved.

Tonight, we're drunk and filled with joy,
    and have the chance at last
to create an uproar, to cry out
    "*hayy o hu*"[1] again and again.

Tonight, with wine we'll wash away
    the intellect's designs
and travel on the feet of love
    to pursue our quest.

Tonight, we've resolved to see
    that Light Bestower to the soul;
We'll journey gracefully,
    like a planet orbiting the sun.

THE WINE-DRENCHED

We, the wine-drenched, are unconscious
    of "we" and "you."[1]
Our hearts are fervent;
    we are immersed in God's love.

Don't speak to us
    about the sober;
we are crazed for God,
    separated from everyone else.

We have no business with anyone
    in the two worlds.
We are not preoccupied with thoughts
    of *how* and *why*.

We are a sea on which
    all that's been discarded can float,
yet, being the ocean of purity,
    we can never be polluted.

Unperturbed by good or bad,
    attached only to the Beloved,
we are waves stirred up in a fervor
    in the sea of fidelity.

We are a friend of the cupbearer
    of the wine house, and flat broke;
we are wrecked and annihilated
    in the tavern of ruin.

Until the sun shines, we will not turn our gaze
    from its direction;
we will climb to every rooftop
    until we see the moon.

GOD-SEEING EYES

Come, I have been freed from
    the bonds of self-worship.
Come, it is the time
    of love and union.

Once I've fashioned you into a mirror
    to reflect the Beloved,
I will give you eyes
    that can see God.

I know the road that those false claimants
    would take you on:
it begins with suffering and leads only
    to more suffering.

Our flower shop is filled with the roses
    of Divine Oneness,
for we have spent a lifetime
    gathering these blooms.

Whatever flower you seek
    can be found in this garden.
Come! You will regret it
    if you wander away.

The flower sold by the hand
    of loving-kindness
deserves to be placed on the breast
    and its fragrance inhaled continuously.

Nurbakhsh has the wealth
    of purity's wares,
while the bankrupt trader in spirituality
    ends up only with his lament.

LOVE

Love is to flee from "I" and "we"[1] and
to rest in the shade of the Friend.

It is to remove oneself from the center and
to pull Him instead to the core of one's soul.

It is to erase one's thoughts and
to tear up the intellect's notebook.

It is to wash one's hands of all but God and
to step back from other doorways.

It is not to read anything but the story of love, and
not to witness anything in the soul but His reflection.

It is not to wish for anything but His company, and
not to hear anything but the words of the Beloved.

It is not to climb on anyone else's rooftop to reach Him, but
to fly continuously towards Him on your own.

It is not to go in search of anyone else, but
to run constantly towards Him alone.

It is to give away Nurbakhsh's heart and soul,
and to receive God in return.

WANDERING SEEKER

O wandering seeker, come
    to this district.
Your Beloved is over here,
    so look this way!

Do not bring "we" and "you"[1] here,
    for it is not allowed in.
Become selfless and uproot
    all thought of self.

If "we" and "you" comes along,
    there will be no news here,
but the moment you become selfless
    receive news and share it with us.

If you take one step in selflessness,
    I will grant your every wish,
but if you still possess "I" and "we"[2]
    then beware of this path!

Arrive humbly and abjectly;
    enter drunkenly.
Abandon your self-existence and
    banish reason from your head.

Come without consciousness of self;
    make sure not to be sober.
Do not see others;
    be mute and deaf as well.

By His beauty, the Beloved will
    bestow light upon you.
Abandon your own sight and
    look with His eyes!

SING THE SONG OF UNITY

Offer up your whole being humbly
    to the wine,
then come to the *khaniqah*
    to discover the mystery.

Drink first with all your soul
    the dregs of the pain of love for Him,
then sing the song of Unity
    in the district of the Beloved.

By praising God, remove from your heart
    the thought of everything else;
become a stranger to yourself and
    make your prayer to Him alone.

When you wish to set foot in
    the circle of *faqr* and *fana*,
leave your self behind and
    abandon illusion.

If the desire for His face exists
    in your heart,
close your eyes to self and
    open them to the Friend.

Regard as a godsend the grace
    of the master's presence;
cut short your speech and extend
    the hand of devotion.

Do not bother the Mahmud of the soul
    with the affairs of state;
sacrifice all to the forelock
    of Ayaz.[1]

If you want your pilgrimage to be accepted
    like that of Nurbakhsh,
abandon Mecca and circle
    the Kaaba of the heart.

BEHOLD!

O Physician of lovers, look at
    this bewildered patient!
I am dying of remorse: come, and
    behold the effect of Your cure!

A lifetime I've pressed my head
    upon Your threshold.
Show compassion and
    save Your destitute one!

You said You would admit anyone
    who turns toward You.
I am burning with love in Your district —
    now, honor Your promise!

Traceless and placeless,
    You have no need.
You are unchanging —
    show consideration for temporal beings!

For how long, O Host, will You continue
    to ignore others?
Look across Your generous banquet table and
    behold the face of Your guest!

I am transient, and unworthy of a relationship
    with the Eternal.
See how remote my despair,
    behold how close Your mercy!

Your tresses cause my unbelief,
    Your countenance my faith;
O You Who exist beyond faith and unbelief,
    behold this believer!

You are the Bestower of light
    on all existence,
the cause of turmoil
    throughout the world.

The people of this world are the ball
    on Your field.
Behold Your polo bat
    and strike!

THE ESSENCE OF CONTENTMENT

You are that being in whom the entire world can be seen;
You are that generosity from which all of existence became manifest.

I am that wave that reaches out to grab Your hem.
You are that ocean in which waves are flowing.

I am that ruined drunkard who is beside himself.
You are that wine that is the object of people's imagination.

I am that mystery that was revealed and became disgraced.
You are that hidden secret in which the world is contained.

I am that word in which meaning cannot be found.
You are that name in which all names and traces are contained.

I am that wandering, whirling atom.
You are that attraction by which this transient world came to exist.

I am that agitated soul that found no rest from self.
You are the very essence of contentment in which all refuge is found.

I am that fable that entertains children.
You are that dot in which a hundred tales are hidden.

I am that one who in this world's sleep is but a dream.
You are that place where all of these "I's" and "we's"[1] continually lament.

"I" AND "YOU"[1]

In pre-eternity
    we all agreed:
that we would never attach our hearts
    to the realm of "I" and "you,"

that we would not get drunk
    from the wine of "I" and "you,"
that we would not become unconscious
    in a stupor of "I" and "you."

The world is but an atom
    in the realm of Being;
notice then how inconsequential
    is the realm of "I" and "you."

Cupbearer, help us, so we can
    become drunk and bewildered,
and break down this fortress
    of "I" and "you."

O hunter, why are you pursuing Him
    with the feet of "I" and "you"?
This prey can never be caught
    by "I" and "you."

The practice of the mind
    is speech; otherwise,
in the school of love there would be
    no talk of "I" and "you."

O Nurbakhsh, as long as
    "I" and "you" remains,
difficult will be the days
    for both I and you.

FIDELITY FROM YOU

You reside in my heart;
    my head desires You.
Night and day I spend
    completely consumed by You.

I have suffered at the hands
    of the people of this age;
in this world I've seen fidelity
    only from You.

We've been completely drunk
    with Your wine since pre-eternity;
we'll remain completely surrendered
    to Your wish till post-eternity.

I've no hope for heaven or
    for the resurrection;
I have never wanted anyone
    but You.

Once I realized that in reality
    the path cannot be traveled
except on Your feet,
    I gave up my own volition.[1]

With every breath I take
    I am conscious of You;
I gave up heart and soul as the price
    of pleasing You.

O Nurbakhsh, because you sacrificed
    your self to God,
people wish to surrender themselves
    to you.

SURRENDER

I saw how good Your pledge was
    in Your faithfulness;
I am content, heart and soul,
    with whatever You wish.

I have surrendered myself and
    all thoughts of possession or lack;
out of desire for You I have cut myself off
    from everyone.

I, like the cup, am delighted with
    whatever You pour in me;
I smile whether You give
    or withhold.

Whatever my heart beholds,
    You are what it sees,
since everything other than You has been erased
    from its view.

Without security my heart risked all
    to buy You with the currency of love;
it had to give the world and all existence
    to meet Your price.

People say that the Kaaba
    is Your abode,
unaware that Your footprint is everywhere
    and You are in everything.

If for years there has been no news
    of Nurbakhsh
it's because he's been residing
    at the threshold of Your palace.

GO!

Go to the circle of love and purity
    wherever it's found;
go and attach yourself to the one
    who takes you from yourself.

Keep away from
    pretension and self-display;
go with sincerity and loyalty to the gathering
    of those with spiritual states.

Don't walk with hypocrites
    and deceitful people;
go with the pain of love to seek
    the one familiar with pain.

Befriend those who have
    no consciousness of self;
go on the path where one doesn't speak
    about "you" and "we."[1]

Do not enter where
    people gossip about others;
go with one who's free
    from such conduct.

The one who speaks of "I" and "you"[2]
    diverts you from the path;
go with those who are
    annihilated from self.

Listen to Nurbakhsh and hear these words
    that spring from love:
"Go to the feast where
    the wine of God's love is served."

HE IS THE LIVING, HE IS THE TRUTH, HE IS *HU* [1]

How lovely, how beautiful
    Your face!
What coyness lies in those eyes
    and eyebrows!

Once I saw
    Your countenance
I could never become intimate
    with anyone else.

I desire only You;
    I utter only Your name.
I see but One, say but One,
    and want but One.

On Your path, I have given up
    both head and soul,
and could never take offense or turn away
    from Your direction.

I embrace both Your grace
    and Your wrath:
for me, Your harshness
    is sweet and pleasant.

I have erased all traces of self
    from my heart's slate,
and in their place have inscribed,
    "Everything is He."

Through Your love
    I have forsaken self-existence
and have become tranquil,
    no longer rushing in every direction.

Whether You bestow light or not,
    all night and day
our *zekr* will be this:
    "He is *Hu*."

GO THERE!

Go wherever the reed player
    of love calls you.
Go wherever you smell the fragrance
    of love and fidelity.

In the realm of love there's no difference
    between *khaniqah* and tavern.
Go to any school that teaches you
    the abandonment of carnal self.

It has never been love's custom
    to wear white.
Follow the path that your heart tells you
    to pursue.

As long as you are trapped in the lasso of "I" and "we"[1]
    you'll remain wretched.
Go and become trapped by the one
    who gives you love and sustenance.

Go and drink that wine that burns
    your self-existence.
Go to the wine seller who's giving away
    the wine of *fana*.

Turn away from the gathering place
    of the self-worshipers.
Go to the tavern that gives away
    wine of love and purity.

The master of love has decreed, "A true human being
    should not be without pain."
Follow the one who gives you
    pain and calamity.

In the gathering of love, don't become careless
    in your service to the cupbearer.
Follow the one who's bestowing wine
    without pretension and ego.

Listen to Nurbakhsh and let go
    of shadows.
Go to the place where the sun bestows
    its loving light.

THE COLORLESS WINE

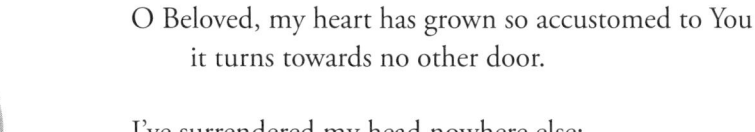

O Beloved, my heart has grown so accustomed to You
    it turns towards no other door.

I've surrendered my head nowhere else;
    I've walked on no other path.

You plundered my heart and faith;
    You ambushed me wherever I went.

I cannot distinguish head from foot;
    I'm but a ball before Your polo bat.

O You, sly Beloved, Your love suffices,
    for there is no friend other than You.

Once I drank the colorless wine
    I became free from the world of colors and scents.

Now I am but a love-crazed soul,
    an enchanted heart crying, "*Hu! Hu!*"

Ever since You bestowed light on my heart,
    it says, "He" at every moment, with no trace of "I."

DON'T GO!

Don't go on any path
    other than the path to God;
with the pain of love, don't approach anyone
    who is not acquainted with pain.

Do not remain bound
    by your ancestors' idol-worship —
become a disciple of God
    and do not obey your own passion.

There are many traps
    set on your path —
Beware of becoming bewitched by the bait
    and don't go without a guide.

Your lusts will take you
    to the path of the carnal self —
don't enter the path of God's friends
    without the aid of love.

The claim, "I am" can be heard
    in every corner of the world —
seek help from God
    and don't go chasing every call.

Go without misgivings where there is selflessness,
    helplessness and self-effacement.
Don't go to the assembly
    of "I" and "you."[1]

Listen to Nurbakhsh and enter the banquet of love
    with sincerity and purity.
Don't go to the assembly
    of the pretentious.

TELL ME

What have I done to make you leave?
    Tell me.
Did you hear offensive words from me?
    Tell me.

You turned me into an idol for yourself.
    That was futile.
Did you experience unfriendliness from me?
    Tell me.

You were a disciple of the master created by
    your own mind;
when you didn't find this idol in me, you went away.
    Isn't that so?

You had come here to increase your
    self-existence;
you didn't buy from me the wares of nothingness.
    Isn't that so?

You thought your sense of "I" and "we"[1]
    would get a boost here;
then you found out that your venture was hopeless.
    Isn't that so?

Your carnal self demanded that you should become
    a shaikh of the path,
but you did not achieve your ego's objective.
    Isn't that so?

The bird of your heart was pursuing
    selfish desires;
that's why you flew away from Nurbakhsh's sanctuary.
    Isn't that so?

DON'T SPEAK

Don't speak of "I" and "you"[1]
    in the banquet of wine-worshipers;
don't speak of yourself
    in the gathering of lovers.

When you sit in the circle of madness,
    be silent;
don't be conscious of your existence and
    don't speak of intelligence and cleverness.

The bird of my heart longs
    for the Friend;
don't speak of the virgins and
    the palaces of paradise.

Don't speak of the fables
    of past events and times
to the one who has turned his back
    on the created world.

Don't speak of the attributes
    of gems and precious stones
to the lover whose ruby-like heart
    is bloodied.

Don't ask about the creed of people of existence
    from those who do not exist;
don't speak of religion, unbelief,
    knowledge and foresight.

Don't ask Nurbakhsh about anything
    other than purity and fidelity;
don't speak to him about people
    who break their vows.

I SAY *HAQQ, HAQQ*, CRY *HU, HU*

As long as any trace of body and soul remains, I say,
    Haqq, Haqq, cry *Hu, Hu*.
Far from any thoughts about this and that, I say,
    Haqq, Haqq, cry *Hu, Hu*.

When the intellectual seeks God,
    he follows his own ego's discourse.
Concealed from the intellect's eyes, I say,
    Haqq, Haqq, cry *Hu, Hu*.

I became a lover, and in this art of loving
    the only problem is "I."
To resolve my dilemma, I say,
    Haqq, Haqq, cry *Hu, Hu*.

Go away mullah, your God is the invention
    of your own mind!
Transcending any understanding and evidence, I say,
    Haqq, Haqq, cry *Hu, Hu*.

O professor, don't try to lecture me about God!
    I do not hear your words.
Beyond any logic and proof, I say,
    Haqq, Haqq, cry *Hu, Hu*.

His love is my guide;
    I have no other leader.
I do not know a settled life; I say,
    Haqq, Haqq, cry *Hu, Hu*.

O hypocritical clergy! I've let go of both your worlds.
    I leave you to your desires.
Not wanting other than the Beloved, I say,
    Haqq, Haqq, cry *Hu, Hu*.

I swing my head and body about;
    I whirl this "I" around
until it falls into the pit of oblivion. I say,
    Haqq, Haqq, cry *Hu, Hu.*

O Nurbakhsh, my tongue is uttering
    a beautiful description of Him.
Listen to what I speak from the bottom of my heart: I say,
    Haqq, Haqq, cry *Hu, Hu*!

THE TALISMAN OF THE SELF

You plundered my broken heart
    and broke apart
my head with the stone
    of desire for You.

Thousands are drenched in blood
    approaching union with You,
heart and soul lost,
    head and feet broken.

Love for Your face has summoned me
    to Divine Unity,
for it has broken both visible
    and hidden idols.

Totally drunk, I burst out
    of self-existence
like a water bubble bursting
    on the ocean.

The cupbearer has sent me
    to the wine vault,
for I've lost my goblet and
    broken my jug.

Perhaps I will see the treasure of the Beloved
    clearly again,
now that my soul has broken
    the talisman of the self.

For you, Nurbakhsh,
    this world has been a dream
by which people are bewitched
    and hearts are broken.

THE NAME OF THE FRIEND

Say continually the name of the Friend,
    slowly, slowly;
with this alchemy change the copper
    of the heart into gold
        slowly, slowly.

Drink from the wine of union
    in the tavern of Unity so that
all thoughts of "we" and "you"[1]
    are removed from your mind
        slowly, slowly.

Stamp your feet on the head of existence,
    empty your hands of both worlds,
then you will become a confidant
    of God's secret
        slowly, slowly.

Follow the path of that king
    who has God's bounty,[2]
and sooner or later he will separate
    you from yourself
        slowly, slowly.

In love's district
    one must not be impatient,
since difficulties will be made easy
    by surrender and contentment
        slowly, slowly.

There are thousands of tests in store
    for a sincere lover
until he can come to know
    love's mystery
        slowly, slowly.

The mystic wayfarer will traverse
    the stations of the path:
he will continue to *baqa*
    after reaching *fana*
        slowly, slowly.

In the school of lovers, silence
    is better than speech.
O Nurbakhsh, the truth of this claim
    was made clear
        slowly, slowly.

WHAT DOES IT MEAN?

You've rushed out of the house utterly drunk — what does it mean?
You've made the whole world anxious — what does it mean?

To behold Your own face again, You've made a mirror;
in the game of love, You've lost to Yourself — what does it mean?

There is none other than You for You to deal with;
You've dealt with Yourself all along — what does it mean?

You are not disturbed that the whole world is watching You;
You've not seen or known other than Yourself — what does it mean?

Everyone's attention is on You, yet with flirtation and coyness
You've ignored everyone — what does it mean?

You set the entire world ablaze and the fire of Your love
melted away the hearts and souls of all — what does it mean?

Through Your grace and purity You've given life to nothingness,
yet in wrath You've drawn the sword of slaughter — what does it mean?

Nurbakhsh, *rend*-like, asks You again,
the banner that You have raised — what does it mean?

SEVERED

My heart is severed
    from both worlds,
from yesterday, today
    and tomorrow.

It has stepped outside the world,
    beyond space,
freed from the bounds of the earth,
    past the Pleiades.

My heart has forgotten the maelstrom
    of "I" and "we";[1]
it has broken its ties
    with everything.

My heart has turned away from all thoughts
    of worldly affairs,
severed its ties with all things
    apparent and hidden.

From one side it has reined in
    vain yearnings,
from the other side it abandoned
    all needs.

My heart has washed its hands of the world
    of happiness and sorrow;
it has cut off the rope
    of pointless desires.

Where has this heart of mine settled?
    I do not know!
It has erased all thoughts except
    the memory of the Friend.

He is the only being existing
    in the world;
He has cut out the tongue of "I" and "we"
    from his chosen few.

O Nurbakhsh, stop talking!
    Those who have heard of
the Friend's attributes have severed
    their ties to the world.

THE NEW YEAR

O people of purity, my heart celebrates
    the new year,
the time for joy, happiness
    and hope.

The eyes that were blinded by
    night's darkness
can now see because
    the sun has risen.

Sing, dance and rejoice like a drunkard,
    for no one
has seen the return
    of a breath already taken.

Yesterday is gone, and there is
    no news of tomorrow;
today is the chosen day and
    the time for joy.

Treasure this new year,
    for a Sufi acquires
the wealth of both worlds
    with one breath.

You are entangled in the trap
    of "I" and "we";[1]
for tranquility of heart, cut yourself off
    from all but the Friend.

If He bestows light,
    your ego will disappear,
just as the bird of my heart
    has flown from its nest.

LA ELAHA ELLA'LLAH[1]

The face of God,
    He, of grandeur:
La elaha ella'Llah

Remembrance at every moment,
    with every breath:
La elaha ella'Llah

No one but He can enter into the sanctuary of
    His essence, source of His attributes:
La elaha ella'Llah

He is in all that appears; He enraptures all realms;
    He is the king of the world of being:
La elaha ella'Llah

Across all the levels of being, He provides drunkenness and wine;
    He is the heart and the heart's beloved:
La elaha ella'Llah

His essence is manifested in all beings;
    He is the light of the sun and the essence of the moon:
La elaha ella'Llah

Creatures in the realm of possibility have come to existence
    through His generosity and the breath of His being:
La elaha ella'Llah

He parades His beauty everywhere in a scandalous guise;
    His name is upon all lips:
La elaha ella'Llah

He knows His own magnificence
    and the boundlessness of His essence:
La elaha ella'Llah

Lovers are drunk from Him;
> mystics are dust at His threshold:
La elaha ella'Llah

Although well-hidden, He is the bestower of light to the soul;
> He is Joseph unseen in the well:
La elaha ella'Llah

FROM TAVERN TO TAVERN

Last night this fine point was explained
    and passed from moth to moth:
that "we" and "you"[1] creates
    fable after fable.

Nothing but the candle must be sought;
    nothing but the candle must be seen.
Thoughts of "I" and "we"[2] do not belong
    in love's district.

Look with the eye of the heart!
    Hidden in your chest is the treasure
that you are seeking as you travel
    from ruin to ruin.

"He is the attractor; He is the attracted.
    He is the seeker; He is the sought."
This statement was passed along in our circle
    from madman to madman.

There is but one wine in the goblet,
    though I have heard it called by
a thousand names while going
    from tavern to tavern.

If you are truly our companion, be valiant
    and pass from this self.
Give up heart and religion at once
    to the Soul of souls.

When love became the architect
    in the Kaaba of our hearts,
an idol-temple was erected
    in every direction.

The light that God bestows He gives
    without asking *how* or *why*.
Why then do you wander uselessly
    from place to place?

TRAVELER ON THE PATH

Have you submitted yourself,
    O traveler on the path?
If not, then look at what you've done
    to be so depressed.

Are you still asking *how* and *why*
    in your mind?
Then you have taken back the head
    you claimed to submit.

Does "I" and "you"[1] still have meaning
    for you?
Then you are still alive and never died
    to yourself.

Do you still do whatever
    you want?
Then you have not cleansed your soul
    of the ego's desire.

Are you still after fame, fortune
    and position?
Then you have not given up
    both worlds.

Is your self-existence still blocking
    your path?
Then you have given your pledge of love
    half-heartedly.

O Nurbakhsh, these travelers
    who are around you
have not become Sufis, but you indulge them
    and count them as such.

THE BROKEN-WINGED BIRD

Who am I?
    A forgotten fable,
a speck of dust left behind by the wind
    in the district of love,

a drunkard who has fallen
    unconscious,
rejected by the master,
    with no guidance,

an exhausted traveler who has lost
    his way,
a refugee worn out
    from suffering and injustice,

a broken-winged bird left behind
    in the cage,
already driven out of the garden and
    ignored by the hunter,

a pale blush on the lips
    of the beloved Shirin,
a smoldering spark left behind
    from the stonecutter Farhad.[1]

Having traded my prayer rug and cloak
    for wine,
I am a hung-over drunk who has forgotten
    all litanies.

Nurbakhsh was drowned
    in the ocean of *fana*,
for he was a muffled sigh in the chest,
    a suppressed cry in the heart.

DISTRICT TO DISTRICT

How can You ever leave my sight —
    when You are the light of my eyes
and have come to rest in the midst of
    my heart and soul?

I have been freed from self —
    with just one glance
You bought my existence
    and I became Your slave.

You are the king of beauty,
    and all hearts are Your captives.
You alone have heard
    this well-sealed secret.

Your Love always
    tears away the veils;
You have split open my heart
    with the arrow of Your eyelash.

O bird of truth still flying
    from district to district,
tell me: have you ever flown
    to any district but His?

Ask the false claimant
    if with his heart's hand
he has ever picked a blossom
    from the garden of love.

Silence, Nurbakhsh, for in the faith
    of the people of heart,
You have chosen the best direction in which to pray:
    towards the Beloved.

HE IS THE ONE, THE ETERNAL, WITHOUT LIKENESS AND ALIVE

O Cupbearer of the soul,
    fill my cup with wine,
let it burn every vein and pore
    of my body.

Let me cry from the bottom
    of my heart, "*Ya Hu!*"
let me shout from the depth
    of my soul, "*Ya Hayy!*"

Let me stamp my foot
    on the head of multiplicity,
let me journey with ease
    on the path of Unity.

This path cannot be traversed
    without wine;
sobriety and the way of madness
    don't go together.

How long do you want to speak
    of the world?
How long do you want to be entrapped
    by your passions?

Leave yourself behind and
    turn to God,
face the sun and
    leave shadows behind.

Let Him bestow light and
    take away the ego,
let the Beloved play the reed-pipe
    of your soul.

THE SOUL OF EXISTENCE

I love existence, for You are
    the soul of existence;
You are visible to me everywhere,
    manifest in every direction.

As long as I am preoccupied with self, I remain
    bewildered, wretched and tormented.
As soon as I am without self, I become joyful,
    for You are the spirit of my soul.

Nothing appears to my eyes and heart
    other than Your face.
You are both apparent in the outward form
    and also hidden within.

You are what is seen by every viewer and
    what is witnessed by every witness.
The form of existence is a manifestation of You.
    You are the being of the cosmos.

Why do rational people try to define You
    through quantity and quality
when You are beyond all thought, opinion
    and even imagination?

The moment I stepped outside the realm
    of "I" and "you"[1]
I clearly saw Your trace everywhere, though in truth
    You remain traceless.

Ever since You bestowed light
    on my wandering heart,
I have come to know that in every realm
    You are my sanctuary and safety.

THE ENDEARING AND LOVING COMPANION

I know that playful coquettish friend,
    it is You.
I know that agreeable loving companion,
    it is You.

The twists and turns of the created world
    are but a fable.
I know the narrator of that tale,
    it is You.

The entire universe is dancing
    to one tune.
I know the composer of that song,
    it is You.

The whole world is perplexed by existence
    and its secret.
I know the source of that mystery,
    it is You.

Everyone is enchanted by the bewitching eyes
    of a sorcerer.
I know the possessor of those beguiling eyes,
    it is You.

In the cradle of existence, from pre- to post-eternity
    is but a moment.
I know that beginning and that end,
    it is You.

I am that featherless, wingless bird
    captured by a hawk.
I know that swift-winged raptor,
    it is You.

From one flirtatious glance, Nurbakhsh became
    your lover and gave up both worlds.
I know the source of that look,
    it is You.

THERE IS NOTHING BUT GOD

There is no one in this world
    other than God.
Do not seek help
    from anyone else.

The whole creation is in need
    of Him;
no one else
    is eternal.

Grab God's garment and ignore
    everything else
so you may receive guidance
    from His grace.

Love is vital to reach the abode
    of the Friend,
for not everyone is worthy
    of this.

You need love to be lost
    in God
and liberated from good and evil,
    right and wrong.

And love will take you away from yourself
    and turn you into Him,
without the aid of talent,
    knowledge and wisdom.

He will take "I" and "we"[1] away
    from your heart
so that the Truth will then bestow light upon it,
    and you'll become the Truth's confidant.

YOU WERE THERE

Wherever I traveled,
    You were manifest;
wherever I looked,
    You were visible.

Whether in idol-temples or the Kaaba,
    synagogues or churches,
I saw people searching for You;
    You were everyone's beloved.

I sought only You in every person I met
    and every place I went;
You were there in every perceptible trace,
    whether on the outside or within.

In the marketplace of love,
    it was revealed
that You were
    both the seller and the buyer.

In every heart whispering of love
    for an idol,
that idol was but a pretext:
    You were both heart and beloved.

From pre- to post-eternity
    throughout the world,
You were all that was hidden or revealed,
    bountiful or scarce.

If You have bestowed light
    and stolen my heart and faith,
this is because You are heart, faith,
    and the illuminator of all light.

LOVE AND LIFE

If you haven't pledged your heart
    to the love of a radiant beauty
consider your life
    a total waste.

The key to eternal life lies
    in the palm of love's hand;
without a discerning beloved,
    one is in reality dead.

If you don't throw your entire being
    before the feet of an idol,
you won't make a profit or grasp
    the treasure of eternal life.

If you do not plant the seed
    of loving-kindness in your heart,
you will never eat any fruit
    from the garden of happiness.

Without love, you have no clue
    about the reason for existence;
without the Beloved, what do you know
    of your purpose in this life?

Not until you become ensnared
    in love's trap will you be free;
trapped in yourself, you remain
    depressed, cold-hearted and miserable.

O my soul, if light is bestowed
    upon your abode,
it is because your heart is bound in love
    to the Beloved.

O PIOUS ASCETIC

O pious ascetic, you lack the sorrow
    of separation from a beloved;
you have nothing to do with the gathering
    of the people of heart.

As long as you retain your prayer beads
    and turban,
you will not feel ashamed
    of "I" and "we."[1]

How can the eye of your heart ever
    be illuminated
if your nights are not darkened
    by His love?

O you who have no commander
    in love,
how will you ever ascend
    the gallows of *fana*?

No lover will ever call you
    free from care
if you do not bear the burden
    of His sorrow in the heart.

If you truly have no secret bond
    with the intellect,
why then do you not relentlessly
    pursue love?

You will be the bestower of light
    to love's display
if for you there is nothing of value
    but love.

THE LOVE-TEACHING GLANCE

Go away pious ascetic.
    In your heart you have
neither burning nor the sighs
    that can ignite fires.

You always look to heaven,
    for in your eyes
you have no
    love-teaching glance.

You have sacrificed head and soul
    to "I" and "we";[1]
you have no hidden teaching
    other than this.

So often are you in mourning
    that you never
have time for festivity and
    new year celebration.

You don't achieve any special grace
    with your night vigils
or from repeating "O God"
    so often.

You have no arrows like ours, which come
    from the sighing quiver of the heart
and which sew shut the mouth
    of the false claimant.

And you, Nurbakhsh,
    your heart is so enamored
from the Beloved's love that you can't tell
    day from night.

LOVE'S BAZAAR

Whoever opens his eyes to You
    loses his blindness.
Whoever finds a place near You
    becomes placeless.

Your face can be seen through
    Your eyes only.
How can anyone observe you
    with his own?

O You, source of desire,
    You are free from all.
What else in all the world
    can anyone yearn for?

Since in love's venture the seller
    is also the buyer,
what use is there in
    trade?

We are the veil covering
    Your face;
You are not hidden and so
    do not need to be found.

Let anyone reveal love's secrets,
    for in Your presence
there is neither confidant
    nor stranger.

O Nurbakhsh, I have taken the blame
    for His sake all my life;
now there is no reason for anyone
    to wish to disgrace me.

THE CIRCLE OF UNITY

As long as you are not bound to a Beloved
> through loving-kindness
your soul will never experience the delight
> of liberation.

Your notebook of knowledge
> is but a toy of your imagination —
reading it in the beginning causes suffering,
> in the end fatigue.

In truth, whatever you see other than love
> is false.
You will never again hear Truth's secret
> this concisely.

Unconsciousness and humility,
> lowliness and nothingness
are a few signs of the lover's
> pre-eminence.

In love's battleground
> the selfless *rend*
receives the rank of commander
> from the Sultan of Beauty.

Cling to the circle of Divine Unity,
> for this solid foundation
grants safety from faltering,
> error and dispersion.

Aided by the heart, we climbed beyond
> the limits of space and creation.
While seated here, we made many journeys
> beyond the horizons.

We drank just a mouthful and
> have remained drunk.
Since the day of the pre-eternal covenant,
> our wine has been perpetually intoxicating.

O Nurbakhsh, I see you are undisturbed
 by the flood of events;
though you may be a drop,
 you are joined with the Ocean.

THE MYSTERIES OF CREATION

O rational one, you do not understand
    the mysteries of creation,
and even if you do know a little,
    you certainly lack complete understanding.

O mullah, you do not go to the mosque
    of your own volition,
but you are unaware of the hand
    that leads you there.

O scholar, your studies of external matters have no end;
    not only do you fail
to understand the outer,
    but you are ignorant of the inner as well.

O lover, you will find
    whatever you wish from your beloved.
You will become united with your love
    but not be conscious of your union.

O traveler, you search in every direction
    for a promising road.
Why do you ask about our state
    when you don't know the heart's language?

O mystic, you see nothing
    but the ocean and the ship.
You have sunk into a whirlpool
    and no longer seek the shore.

O Nurbakhsh, in peace you have been liberated
    from all this turmoil;
no longer do you know the state of those
    with darkened days and feet stuck in the mud.

WHAT DO YOU KNOW?

What do you know of the stricken heart's burning
    and how it feels?
Though you've heard about God,
    what do you know of Him?

We've never revealed our thoughts
    to you.
When you don't know our secret,
    what can you know of us?

You have not taken one step on the path
    of love and purity.
What can you know of the station of *baqa*
    when you have not reached *fana*?

Drunk with "we" and "you,"[1] how can you
    gain any news of Him?
What can you know of fidelity
    when you flee harshness?

You have not given up your mind and soul
    to a beloved,
so what can you know about the lover's
    helpless state?

You delude yourself that you're traveling
    the way to God,
but what do you know of this
    endless path?

You're but a child riding your skirt like
    a make-believe horse.
What do you know of the path,
    the wayfarer and the guide?

Though you may have caught a few words
    from Nurbakhsh,
what do you know of the pain and burning
    of the love-struck heart?

THE TAVERN'S PROSPERITY

Cupbearer, pour wine!
    What is the delay?
Why do You hesitate to do
    good deeds?

Since the lovers' affairs are in
    Your hands,
be gracious! Why are You
    deliberating?

You keep the inner state of
    an entire people in ruin
and still You exempt Yourself
    from accusations and blame.

When You are ruining the tavern's prosperity
    with these dealings,
do You know what you are doing
    to the master?

Our cry has reached to the placeless
    all because of You,
yet You nonchalantly blame it all
    on fate.

The novices are caught up
    in their immature thoughts.
Why do You give form
    to such crude imaginations?

Since you know that the Cupbearer's delay
    is for the best,
why then, Nurbakhsh, do you keep up
    this pointless complaining?

TO WHOM ARE YOU PRAYING?

No matter how much I plead with You,
    still You remain aloof.
O my great fortune,
    why do You prolong this tale?

You have set out on a journey —
    I have no complaint.
You are a flash of the Truth;
    You abandon illusion.

The place of the manifestation of Your truth
    is nowhere but in our unreal world.
If we do not put up with Your coyness,
    with whom then will You flirt?

I exclaimed, "O hope of hearts,
    I will give up my soul on Your path."
He answered, "This pleading of yours
    is worth nothing to Me."

I said to Him, "From Your amorous gesture
    a world was thrown into temptation."
He replied, "Be silent! You are revealing
    the secret to the whole world."

O hypocritical, blathering mullah,
    stop your sarcasm about my unbelief
or I'll reveal to whom
    you are really praying!

The Beloved is in your house —
    what excuse do you have
for turning away from our Bestower of light
    to face Mecca instead?

THE SOURCE OF JOY

I will not turn my heart from You,
    for You're the source of my joy.
While You are present,
    I am unaware of myself.

In myself, I am nothing
    but darkness.
You are my light; You are the being
    of my visible form.

Evidence for my existence lies in
    my closeness or distance from You.
Yet now that I cease to exist,
    You become my closeness, my distance.

Where are You not present that I should
    need to seek You out?
Whichever path I take
    You are there along the way.

Sama is the practice of lovers
    in separation:
with every breath, You bestow sustenance
    and rapture.

I've sold paradise, with all its palaces and virgins,
    for a grain of barley;
You are my paradise,
    my palaces and virgins.

Erase the notebook of knowledge —
    then, like Nurbakhsh, say,
"O my Beloved, You are my holy scripture,
    the Book of Psalms that I sing."

LOVE IS SWEET

Servanthood is easy
    if you are free;
love is sweet
    if you become a lover.[1]

As long as you are still learning,
    do not seek to instruct;
students will arrive
    once you become a teacher.

You will see the Friend's splendor
    in every direction
if you are guided
    on love's path.

Yes, it is possible to affirm
    loving-kindness
if you are joyful
    in your self-negation.

Your nourishment will come
    from love's breast
if you are reborn into the world
    of love.

You will lose
    your integrity
if you become attached to those
    gathered around you.

O Nurbakhsh, in the end your being will
    become realized only in non-existence,
even if you become a teacher
    to the perfected ones.

MISCONCEPTION

Blood rains from my eyes
    for neither tears nor sighs remain.
How strange that for me everything has come to depend
    upon a smile, a glance.

These crude imaginings, these incessant thoughts —
    all were traps.
Gone now, they did not lead
    to inner awakening.

To whom can I speak of this misconception?
    It is a serious mistake
to believe that the nightingale's cry
    is from desire for the face of the rose.

He who opens his mouth and declares,
    "I am a lover"
is not sincere in love
    and will never reach the goal.

Disregard the physical form!
    Barter away heart and religion!
Choose instead a beautiful idol
    of perfect royal splendor.

Sit with tight lips and
    keep silent!
Put aside intellect, judgment and awareness;
    do not seek a path!

If He should give you good news
    that you have arrived at some destination,
disregard it!
    Have no hope of it!

By relying in this way
    on the help of love and drunkenness,
at every moment — not just now and then —
    you will become free of self-worship.

WHETHER YOU LIKE IT OR NOT

You are my heart and my beloved,
    whether You like it or not.
You are my knowing idol,
    whether You like it or not.

How can I complain about You
    when You are entirely kindness and grace?
You enliven my marketplace,
    whether You like it or not.

You're all love and fidelity,
    all bliss and purity.
O my idol, You're my beloved,
    whether You like it or not.

I have fallen on Your path;
    I've been made drunken by Your glance.
You desire me,
    whether You like it or not.

What transgression? What blame?
    What merit? What punishment?
You've got to put up with me,
    whether You like it or not.

Since You're the wayfarer and the path,
    whether I like it or not,
You're my leader and commander,
    whether You like it or not.

You're my patience, my peace:
    all I possess is You.
You're the source of my nourishment,
    whether You like it or not.

Nurbakhsh has come to You
    demanding to see Your face,
for You owe him this much,
    whether You like it or not.

THE DISPLAY OF CREATION

Since I see You want me to be crazy,
    I've fallen into madness and disgrace.
I burn in Your candle's flame, knowing
    that You want me to be a moth.

Neither an intellectual, nor a lover — who am I?
    You know that I am nothing,
and that sometimes You want a friend,
    sometimes a stranger.

Who should I seek? Where should I go?
    I know and I say:
You Yourself are both Layli and Majnun,
    while You want me to be but a fable.

You are both pain and cure,
    the wealth of my soul —
O my hidden treasure, why do You want
    to turn me to ruins?

You are my wish and desire —
    who else can I long for?
Tell me what you want from me
    by demanding in a *rend*-like way.

The display of creation became a trap
    on the path of those who yearn for You.
I no longer see any prey that would lead me to think
    that you desire some bait.

O Nurbakhsh, other than regret,
    what have you gained from your self,
as sometimes you wander in the wilderness
    and sometimes desire a home?

THE DROP AND THE OCEAN

As long as you remain a prisoner of yourself,
    you will be a drop, not the Ocean.
Remove the veil of self, and you'll see that
    you are the same water.[1]

People's acceptance has driven you
    away from God.
Not until you've been completely disgraced
    will you be allowed to enter the tavern of ruin.

If you truly desire Him,
    don't follow your own desires.
You cannot exist for Him
    if you exist for yourself.

Seek your God, for life
    is passing you by.
You're still worshiping
    your ancestors' idols.

Stop pursuing your own wishes
    if you want union with Him.
What is the gain when every moment
    you are attached to a different desire?

Only after having attained *fana*
    will you attain *baqa*.
To affirm God
    you must first negate your self.

Like Nurbakhsh, throw yourself
    into the ocean of *fana*,
Then witness with the eye of the Ocean
    that you are indeed that very Ocean.

THE CRAZY INTELLECT

Through love, I have reached a place
    where no trace of love remains,
where "I" and "we"[1] and the image of existence
    have all been forgotten in yearning.

Where am I now? Who can know anything,
    here where no knowledge, no judgment can be found?
In His presence, even love is bewildered
    and the intellect is crazy, talking nonsense.

I am just a traceless dervish:
    helpless and without self,
free from concern about fidelity or harshness,
    a stranger to family and acquaintances.

Only for this can I still be blamed —
    that a cry comes from within me:
out of regret for Nurbakhsh, I say,
      "You have gone, and I don't know where you are."

HE IS, THERE IS NOTHING BUT HE

Since *Hu* never displayed His visage to anyone,
    nobody ever spoke about *Hu*.
The God of the hidden and the revealed
    declared this from His Essence to His friends:
      He is, there is nothing but He.

I passed by the tavern,
    free from the chatter of strangers.
An intoxicated wise one was drunkenly singing,
    "There is nothing in our goblet but Him."
      He is, there is nothing but He.

Like a mystic, I searched in the temple
    and saw a fire burning within.
The master of the holy fire eased my concern by saying,
    "He is the goal; fire and smoke are just pretexts."
      He is, there is nothing but He.

I passed next to the prayer niche of the mosque
    to seek an answer about Him from the imam.
"Leave behind both right and wrong," he replied,
    "Then you will witness directly."
      He is, there is nothing but He.

I went to the priest in the church
    to ask him to explain the riddle of the trinity.
"Do not sting this already wounded heart,
    for only the One is intended by three," he said.
      He is, there is nothing but He.

An idol worshiper, bewildered at the idol's foot,
    hands crossed on his breast and heart filled with cries,
was admitting openly as tears poured from his eyes,
    "You are but a symbol; He is the object of worship."
      He is, there is nothing but He.

A lover set afire by the plundering of love,
    his face awestruck by love's royal game,[1]
his body gaunt due to love's soul-consuming flames —
    these were his only words: "Everything other than Him is false."
    He is, there is nothing but He.

A brazen beauty had taken harp in hand
    and drunkenly played upon its strings.
I asked, "How do you think of Him?"
    She struck up a tune and answered,
      "*He is, there is nothing but He.*"

Bewildered, a philosopher sat in a corner
    pondering the mystery of life and death.
When I questioned him about some subtle point,
    he replied, "All thought about Him is useless."
    He is, there is nothing but He.

I found a mystic whose heart was enlightened
    and asked him to speak of the Friend.
"Rise and look to the meadow's edge," he said,
    "Both rose and nightingale have opened their lips in song."
    He is, there is nothing but He.

Oneness[2] is His sign,
    Unicity[3] is His explanation,
"Say, He is Allah" is His language.
    Because of Him the lord of love is the bestower of light.
    He is, there is nothing but He.

MY NEW YEAR[1] IS YOU

O You, companion of all my moments,
    You are the tranquility of the entire world.
Light and joy, refuge and sanctuary —
    all are You.

You are my sorrow's confidant,
    You are strength and power.
You are beyond comparison,
    above anything I can say.

My new year is You, my festival, You,
    the delight of my soul is You.
You are my beloved, my only love;
    You are my very soul.

O my elegant cypress, all my patience
    and peacefulness come from You.
You are my profit and gain,
    what I possess or lack.

I'd give up my soul to You if only
    You would rest Your foot on my head;
It doesn't matter how much disdain You show
    or that You regard me as worthless.

My new year is You, my festival, You,
    the delight of my soul is You.
You are my beloved, my only love;
    You are my very soul.

You belong to the people of purity.
    No — You are purity itself.
You are bound by fidelity.
    No — You're the very embodiment of fidelity.

I am a lover of pain;
    You are my pain and affliction,
I am slain by love;
    You are the physician, and my only cure.

My new year is You, my festival, You,
    the delight of my soul is You.
You are my beloved, my only love,
    You are my very soul.

On the path of devotion,
    You are both disciple and master.
In the rulebook of loving-kindness
    You are both the ink and what is written.

The moment that You generously
    entered into my heart
You became the hope filling my chest
    and the remembrance always on my mind,

My new year is You, my festival, You,
    the delight of my soul is You.
You are my beloved, my only love,
    You are my very soul.

THE MASTER'S GRACE

My heart is caught in His lasso
    and cannot be still.
If it does not perish in this condition,
    it's because of the master's grace.

Pain from Him is its own cure.
    The heart will burn as long as
the flames continue; if they do,
    it's because of the master's grace.

O God, make me more of a lover.
    Don't let me get sober.
Believe me, if I'm sincere,
    it's because of the master's grace.

I don't seek drunkenness.
    I have nothing but *faqr*.
If I lose my existence,
    it's because of the master's grace.

I will cut through wisdom
    and go completely mad.
If I become estranged from the world,
    it's because of the master's grace.

I am a lover afflicted with pain,
    freed from the bodily form.[1]
If, in short, I bear no fruit,
    it's because of the master's grace.

I am a wretched beggar,
    in love with pain and calamity.
If I am afflicted with His love,
    it's because of the master's grace.

His love is the hope of my life;
    it's my heart's comfort and security.
If my heart knows nobody but Him,
    it's because of the master's grace.

If my heart has abandoned me
    and flown from my rooftop
to settle in His district,
    it's because of the master's grace.

My heart circles around His district
    and beholds His loving face.
If I desire Him in every moment,
    it's because of the master's grace.

I am both candle and moth,
    treasure and ruin.
If I am a stranger to myself,
    it's because of the master's grace.

I am a beggar for His love;
    day and night I am beside myself.
If I cry out in praise of His beauty,
    it's because of the master's grace.

The heart's fire is kindled;
    it's burning away "I" and "you."[2]
If any false claims are consumed,
    it's because of the master's grace.

I do not desire other than Him.
    If He casts His glance at me for a moment
and I become the bestower of light to the sun and moon,
    it's because of the master's grace.

HU, HAQQ

Every moment I will face His direction
and direct my heart towards Him,
grow accustomed to feeling pain from love for Him
and like the screech owl[1] constantly call out to God.
    I will say *Haqq, Haqq,* cry *Hu, Hu,*
    until I turn "I" and "we"[2] into Him.

I am the goblet, He is my wine;
I am the reed-flute, He is the breath that plays me.
His essence is existence, while I am non-existent;
I am transient, while He is eternal.
    I will say *Haqq, Haqq,* cry *Hu, Hu,*
    until I turn "I" and "we" into Him.

I am the worshiper, He is the object of worship;
I bow in adoration, He is the one adored.
I am the wayfarer and He is my goal;
I am the appearance, while He is True Being.
    I will say *Haqq, Haqq,* cry *Hu, Hu,*
    until I turn "I" and "we" into Him.

I am a thorn, while He is a rose bough;
I am a particular, while He is Universal Being.
I am a cup, while He is the wine-serving cupbearer;
He is the lute that leads the tune of creation, while I am the drum.
    I will say *Haqq, Haqq,* cry *Hu, Hu,*
    until I turn "I" and "we" into Him.

I am a clueless seeker, trying to point the way,
while He is the leader and majestic path.
I am a bird without wings or feathers,
while He is the sky above the land and sea.
    I will say *Haqq, Haqq,* cry *Hu, Hu,*
    until I turn "I" and "we" into Him.

I am an atom, while He is the universe to me;
I am a drop, while He is the ocean to me.
I am the servant, while He is my master;
I am negated, while He is the one I affirm.
    I will say *Haqq, Haqq,* cry *Hu, Hu,*
    until I turn "I" and "we" into Him.

I am the seeker, while He is the one sought;
I am the desirer, while He is the one desired.
I am the lover, while He is the beloved;
I am the drunkard, while He is the one causing commotion.
> I will say *Haqq, Haqq,* cry *Hu, Hu,*
> until I turn "I" and "we" into Him.

I am the prey, while He is the hunter;
I am the captive, while He is free.
I am a ruin, while He is thriving;
I am Majnun, while He is Farhad.[3]
> I will say *Haqq, Haqq,* cry *Hu, Hu,*
> until I turn "I" and "we" into Him.

He is the vat-house, while I am the wine cup;
He is the enchanter, while I am the fable.
He is all awareness, while I am crazed;
He is the candle's flame, while I am the moth.
> I will say *Haqq, Haqq,* cry *Hu, Hu,*
> until I turn "I" and "we" into Him.

I have lost my heart, while He is my heart's beloved;
I am a soldier, while He is my general.
I am grieving and He is my consolation;
I have no one else — He is my only friend.
> I will say *Haqq, Haqq,* cry *Hu, Hu,*
> until I turn "I" and "we" into Him.

I am poor and my days are dark;
He is the radiant sun of guidance.
I am an atom that reflects light,
while He is the bestower of light to all creation.
> I will say *Haqq, Haqq,* cry *Hu, Hu,*
> until I turn "I" and "we" into Him.

SAMA

It's the time of *sama*!
Clap your hands happily!
All who have escaped from self
will get drunk tonight!
        It is God's decree!
        Allah! Allah!

How long will you sit
and suffer in seclusion?
Rise on the feet of aspiration
and turn towards service instead.
        It is God's decree!
        Allah! Allah!

Rise and beat the frame drum!
Come, join the ranks!
Clap your hands drunkenly!
Now make a target of your self.
        It is God's decree!
        Allah! Allah!

Humbly and with love
you may escape
from the bonds of existence
and self-worship!
        It is God's decree!
        Allah! Allah!

Spend this moment in pure joy,
observe love and good faith.
Pledge your very existence,
annihilate your self in God!
        It is God's decree!
        Allah! Allah!

The lover is silent,
with no intellect or consciousness.
He has been bubbling within like a vat of wine.
It is time now to roar!
> It is God's decree!
> *Allah! Allah!*

If you are discerning,
then seize upon this moment,
for this transitory life
lasts only a short while.
> It is God's decree!
> *Allah! Allah!*

In the proximity of the Beloved,
do not bother with cures;
freely offer up
your distracted soul!
> It is God's decree!
> *Allah! Allah!*

We worship wine.
As long as we exist,
we are drunk and delivered
from our selves.
> It is God's decree!
> *Allah! Allah!*

We are light-headed,
drinkers of the dregs.
We have no distinct features;
we behave as Sufis.
> It is God's decree!
> *Allah! Allah!*

Where are You, O Beloved?
Have You no concern for us?
We are just beggars
looking for provisions.
        It is God's decree!
        Allah! Allah!

You are the soul's nourishment;
You are the heart's serenity.
You are both pain and cure;
You are both grace and what is given.
        It is God's decree!
        Allah! Allah!

شنوا یی

Masnavis

THE TAVERN OF RUIN

There is no path to God through prayer;
the path to the Truth leads from the tavern of ruin.

Prayers, supplications, litanies and remembrances
all keep you busy behind the Beloved's door.

As long as you call upon Him, you are an idol-worshiper;
if you really want Him, you must be totally drunk.

As long as you see the path, and yourself as a traveler, you're an outsider,
you are a prisoner of your own ego, engaged in self-deception.

If you are preoccupied with your intellect and the created world,
it is difficult for you to see Reality.

Like a *rend* step into the tavern of ruin
and drunkenly unburden yourself of all your adornments.

In this way you can see God through God's eyes,
for how can the limited see the Absolute?

The tavern's resident is a stranger to himself;
he is a madman in the eyes of rational people.

The tavern's resident has become purged of self altogether;
there is nothing in his head and chest other than God.

The tavern's resident is beyond good and evil;
he is beyond the realm of intellect and madness.

The tavern's resident is beyond unbelief and religion;
he is not preoccupied with the book of the lost and the saved.

The tavern's resident never sees the creation;
he does not think of union and separation.

The tavern's resident dwells in placelessness;
his only trace is his tracelessness.

The tavern's resident is not concerned with "I" and "you";[1]
he has gone beyond "there is no god" and resides in "only God."[2]

The tavern's resident is hidden from his own eyes;
he does not think about having more or reflect on possessing less.

The tavern's resident has no religion or belief;
for him there is no difference between salve and sting.

The tavern's resident is beyond both worlds;
his residence is under the shelter of God.

O Nurbakhsh, stop these ravings and this incoherent speech —
No one but God knows of the tavern of ruin.

REASON AND LOVE

Reason says, "I am the proof for every phenomenon."
Love replies, "I am the king of all existence."

Reason says, "I am aware of all good and evil."
Love replies, "I travel far beyond these."

Reason says, "I am the guide to the way of being."
Love replies, "I am the trailblazer towards non-being."

Reason says, "I am the custodian of existence."
Love replies, "I am free from existence and non-existence."

Reason says, "I am the law that governs the firmament."
Love replies, "I have transcended the limits of dimensions."

Reason says, "I am a king who has won many battles."
Love replies, "I am the ruler of hearts and souls."

Reason says, "I read about the discoveries of all things intelligible."
Love replies, "I know the science of the unknown."

Reason says, "I save everyone from danger."
Love replies, "I am safe in the midst of danger."

Reason says, "I am the guide who is knowledgeable about the path."
Love replies, "I am on the path that leads to a place with no address."

Reason says, "I am the symbol of honor."
Love replies, "I am traceless and as low as dust."

Reason says, "I am learned and have attained many things."
Love replies, "I am in pursuit of union alone."

Reason says, "I am clever and have many talents."
Love replies, "I have nothing to do with your talents."

Reason says, "I am well-informed and highly educated."
Love replies, "I know nothing of this and that."

Reason says, "I engage in debates and argumentation."
Love replies, "I am involved only with ecstasy and spiritual states."

Reason says, "I am the lamp for the wretched."
Love replies, "I am the light bestower who sets hearts on fire."

THE SUFIS' *SAMA*

Let go of yourself in the Sufis' *sama*;
abandon every thought and venture.

Clear from your head all perception of self;
put in shackles all desire, shrewdness and cleverness.

This is the retreat of love, don't ever forget!
Make yourself crazy! Don't remain sane!

The Sufis' uproar burns away self-existence;
their fervor, ecstasy and rapture ignite the heart.

Pass beyond consciousness of self so that you may see God;
open the heart's eye so that you may see purity!

Here is the feast of those drunk with God;
here is the assembly of peace and fidelity.

Let out a drunken roar without sense of self;
give up your heart, spirit and head in the Beloved's sanctuary.

Offer your heart in the marketplace of love —
God is the buyer of love here.

Keep knocking on the door until you hear a response;
shout until you find the door open!

This is the feast of *sama* and the gathering of the *rendan*.
If your goal is to see God, here is your opportunity.[1]

OPENING TO *SAMA*

The *sama* of the Sufis springs out of love for the Beloved,
for their hearts are restless with yearning for Him.

If you are one of God's drunkards, get up and clap your hands,
stamp your feet and beat the drums.

Leave behind your prudent intellect and rise to your feet;
let go of yourself and embrace the drunkards.

Such is the state and condition of the sincere —
full of lovers' fervor and song.

Enter now the banquet of *sama* with drum and reed flute;
cry out, shout and roar!

May you forget your self and submerge
into the sea of Unity dead drunk.

May you become empty of yourself and full of Him,
singing drunkenly His names: *Haqq, Haqq* and *Hu, Hu*.

HE

When someone enters God's assembly on the feet of sincerity,
all his existence follows his heart.

He hangs neediness on the tall gallows,
annihilates himself for the Friend and vanishes altogether.

He pours down God's wine of Unity into the goblet of his being,
takes "I" and "you"[1] and turns them into "He"!

By the decree of the heart, he is liberated from the confines of the ego;
he removes the veil of "we" and "you"[2] and becomes God.

He is no longer a traveler on the path,
    but a lover with no religion and a lost heart.
His existence and non-existence are now merged with the light of the Friend.

His eyes become illuminated with the light bestowed by God.
No longer is there other than Him; no longer is there "I" in sight.

THE DOG

There was once a grief-stricken, good-natured, ragged man
who was accompanied at all times by a dog.

Wealth and position did not concern him;
he took refuge in nothing and no one.

He was never worried in the least about food,
and would only open his mouth to beg food for his dog.

Someone remarked, "O you at war with this world,
don't disgrace yourself for the sake of a dog.

You who are God-like in your freedom from need,
why beg for the benefit of a dog?"

When the pain-afflicted one heard these words,
he responded with sighs of anguish:

"If I were to turn away from this friend,
there would be no one left to love me.

In loyalty, dogs are superior to humans.
They are better friends than all these disloyal people."

SEA WAVE

Your heart's desire is not a worthy master;[1]
the core of your heart is not that deep.

What could your heart want when it has nothing,
lacking discernment of the outer and the inner dimensions?

What is your heart that it should assert its self-existence,
worshiping itself through its thoughts?

A mere bubble on water, what of its psyche?[2]
What can it accomplish, and what of its strength?

Your heart is like a wave in the sea of existence;
it rises and falls through the motion of the sea.

How can the wave know anything of the sea?
Its vision is so limited that it can't tell up from down.

It eventually lays its head in the bosom of the sea
as if it never existed at all.

Before it has a chance to lift up its head
another wave comes crashing towards it.

This clashing of waves gives rise to "we" and "you,"[3]
each wave now attracted to this, now running away from that.

It fosters this imagination in its mind
until it is consumed by the sea.

What a sea, what a deep and vast sea!
No one knows it or can describe it.

What strength, what power, what meaning, what wisdom!
What beginning, what end, what cause, what effect!

Except silence you have no answer
with which to veil your ignorance.

Wave, give up this self-centeredness
and like us dip your head in Unity's sea.

Abandon your combative, vengeful disposition,
your jealousy, crookedness and destructive temper.

Learn love, loyalty, and purity;
gladden for a moment a poor heart.

Practice loving-kindness, for that way,
once you are free from consciousness of self, you will be able to see God.

THE ILLUSION OF "I" AND "YOU"[1]

O You, Whose Being is the source of all existence,
we would be destitute without You.

With You I am above all that exists;
without You, who am I? Nothing!

In this twisted and convoluted world,
You are my beginning and my end. I am nothing.

Believe me when I tell You that I am bewildered —
O my existence, without You I am less than nothing.

This illusion of "I" and "you" was only a dream;
anything other than You is only a mirage.

What can I say? You transcend all words;
You are beyond letters, sounds and any poem of mine.

It is best if I keep my lips sealed and not utter a word,
for You are all that exists and I, just an illusion.

THE IMAGE OF EXISTENCE

Come, so we can wash away the image of existence
    and no longer speak of "I" and "we."[1]

Come, and like us eliminate your thoughts,
    forget both worlds and be silent.

Come, shun the shame of knowing
    and remove all learning from your head.

Come, so we can transcend what can be said
    and blind our eyes to all there is to see.

Come, we will be strangers to all
    and seem mad in the eyes of the rational.

Come, and we'll empty ourselves of self
    and leave behind the disgrace of "I."

Come, so we can welcome unfulfillment
    and banish self-interest from our hearts.

Come, let's drown in the Ocean of Unity,
    free from all thoughts of union and separation,

as this world, which is no more than what is old and what is new,
    is not even worth a grain of sand.

LISTEN TO GOD

Listen to God as He tells a story;
He gives guidance to those who gamble all for love.

He says: First of all, I burned you up,
then I taught you the way of loving.

To see the image of My own face,
I manifested My own form.

From the first, My love guided you
until the practice of loving was fully realized.

In pre-eternity I set the trap of love
so that I might cause you to love Me.

No one can be a lover until I want it,
nor can one sincerely love Me unless I desire it.

There can be no Beloved unless there is a lover;
there must be an attractor for one to be attracted.

❖ ❖ ❖ ❖

As soon as I found you worthy of Me
I started the ferment of love in your heart.

First, love makes you crazy
and estranges you from "I" and "we."[1]

As you make the journey through the twists and turns of love,
awareness of everything else is driven from your being.

When love comes to settle in your breast,
it confounds and humiliates the intellect.

You become free from all being and non-being,
free from the bonds of self-display.

Love is not tamed by every ruffian and rascal;
God's trap does not ensnare unworthy people.

This feast from the unseen is fit only for the valiant;
not every heart is worthy of divine beneficence.

Love cannot go hand-in-hand with lust;
the immature are not worthy companions for the mature.

What has love to do with unbelief or faith?
What has love to do with paradise or hell?

Love makes those who gamble all away its fair game;
it is not interested in hunting good-for-nothings.

Only those whose hearts are alive become drunk on love.
How could those with deadened hearts ever realize love?

Love trades with non-being alone.
As long as you still exist, how can there be love?

Love seeks a contender who has thrown care to the winds,
who is not afraid of being annihilated.

Love brings your intellect to heel, so that
no questioning may remain in your heart.

If love is fully established in your breast, then set out
for the valley of *faqr* and *fana*.

Be a lover, be mad, lose consciousness of self!
Be a Sufi in the ranks of the liberated!

❖ ❖ ❖ ❖

Who is the lover? Nothing. Not even a mirage.
There's not even a trace of him on the water.

In both worlds, for him the Beloved suffices;
everyone else is a stranger to him.

In his world there is only the Beloved;
the only passion in the lover's heart is the passion for Him.

Whatever the Beloved wants is fine with him;
he desires only what the Beloved desires.

If desire for union fills your head, that is merely passion;
this approach leads to a different path.

The lover wants only what the Beloved wants;
it is something beyond personal desire.

Lovers are not involved with the ego;
the lover's heart contains the Beloved alone.

The love-crazed lover doesn't know who he is;
although he appears to be, in fact he really is not.

To say "I love you," is itself a claim,
a claim that is invalid and out of place.

Whoever expresses love before the Beloved
is trying to manipulate the course of love.

How can you claim to be a lover through your carnal self?
Forget yourself if you are a sincere seeker!

Never desire anything from your Beloved;
do not make an appeal, even in looking!

Before His face, you should stitch the eyes of existence shut;
if you still exist, you are a non-believer in love.

The Beloved is all, and the lover is not;
the Beloved is alive, and the lover is dead.

❖ ❖ ❖ ❖

Who is the Beloved? The One Who burns up your being
and teaches you the method of non-existence.

Who is the Beloved? The One Who makes you selfless,
the One Who separates you from all fear and apprehension.

Who is the Beloved? The One Who makes you free
from the noose of the self and brings joy to your heart.

Who is the Beloved? The One Who makes you lose yourself,
the One Who casts you into the vat of Unity.

❖ ❖ ❖ ❖

No one but God is such a beloved;
In reality, this is God's word, nothing else.

Devote your heart to a master who is aware;
consign your self to the flames of God's fire.

To find the heart-sought end,
seek out a traveler who truly knows the path.

To reach the Kaaba of *faqr* and *fana*,
follow him on the feet of submission and contentment.

If you don't you'll wander down dead-end paths,
and become indebted to those who are ignorant.

In such circles lurk monsters and the abyss;
so be careful, for the path is hard.

LOVE AND THE HEART

Listen to the heart as it tells a tale:
how could one who is content with God complain?

He speaks of submission and contentment,
not of possessing more or less.

His every moment is full of joy,
for at every instant he is with God.

❖ ❖ ❖ ❖

Complaining of separation is a sign of self-involvement;
"near" and "far" are terms invented by cunning reason.

The heart purified of everything becomes the place of God;
such a heart exists within the friends of God.

How could a heart freed of the self's deceit
ever think of prison and liberty?

How could a real heart ever become disturbed?
How could it ever become weary of separation?

How could a heart overcome with love for the Glorious God
have room for anything that is other than the Truth?

The heart that is smitten with God loses its self;
one who has become a Sufi loses his heart.

One who is a Sufi has no desires;
desires are for those who are insincere.

Seek a heart, O you prisoners of the self,
that you may reach the station of security.

What you call the "heart" is really your carnal self,
subject day and night to fear and hope.

What you call the "heart" is nothing but the passions,
which cause you to have regrets and expectations.

What you call the "heart" is really the cunning intellect,
which is imprisoned in the grip of "I" and "we."[1]

What you call the "heart" is really your desires,
which exert their influences on both your words and deeds.

❖ ❖ ❖ ❖

The heart is the mirror of the Lord;
how could anything other than Him become settled there?

The heart sees only Unity;
it is freed from perceiving separate things.

The eye of the heart sees with certainty that everywhere
there is only one Being, in both this world and the hereafter.

The heart perceives unbelief in others as faith;
the heart sees offense by others as kindness.

The one who still feels offense has no heart;
the one who still sees bad in things has no heart.

Whatever may happen is good for those of heart;
whatever is said by one with heart is good.

Those of heart do not speak with an acid tongue;
their speech is like a salve.

The heart is the first stage of Unity,
for it is detached from the realm of matter and multiplicity.

The thing in your breast that you name the "heart" is no heart;
that's merely what ordinary people mean by "heart."

The heart has no limit, it is infinite;
that is why it is called the "Throne of God."

This material organ that can be replaced,
that can be serviced and repaired,

how could it be the heart of those of heart?
How could it represent God's throne?

Abandon this patent superstition!
The thing that fills the chest's cavity is not the heart!

No one knows the extent of the heart
that serves as the abode of God.

The heart bestows purity on Adam's soul,
the soul that rules over the world.

It's not easy to reach the station of the heart;
it is difficult to arrive at that stage.

As long as you are obsessed by "I" and "we,"
the heart will have nothing to do with you.

As long as your intellect guides your soul,
how can you begin to know the heart?

❖ ❖ ❖ ❖

To reach the heart you must have a master;
to reach its district you must possess love.

You must offer up your head in the way of the master
if you are to be led by him on this path.

To give up one's head is not in everyone's capacity;
surrendering the self is not for every rascal.

Giving heart and soul to someone is not just talk;
not everyone is fit to embrace this undertaking.

Of the thousands who become Sufis
few are so yielding as to give up their selves.

Many a one, motivated by desire,
has called himself a Sufi to show off.

Many a one has become a Sufi
in order to show that he is someone important.

There's many a one ruled by the intellect
who becomes a Sufi purely in name

in order to learn the Sufis' secrets
so he may, in turn, reveal them to others,

thereby becoming known as a sage
and gratifying the base self that rules him.

There is one who becomes a Sufi
that he may be supported by others.

He has a dependent personality,
becoming a Sufi without understanding.

To acquire peace of soul,
he becomes a simpleminded Sufi.

Another becomes a Sufi without hesitation or doubt,
seeking the mysteries of the unseen.

Another sincerely becomes a Sufi,
so that his sickness may be cured.

Another becomes a Sufi out of despair
over the loss of all that he has possessed.

Out of thousands, few become real Sufis;
the others only pretend to be such.

❖ ❖ ❖ ❖

If you're to travel this endless path,
your heart must be guided by love.

Few fall heart and soul into the trap of love;
few are given the chance of a lifetime to drink from the cup of love.

What others call "love" is no more than desire;
one is to the other like a phoenix to a fly!

Those moved by desire become Sufis just in name
and after a while go off another way.

Moved by desire each new day,
they invent a hundred pretexts to follow a different master.

Moved by desire, their heads a-buzz,
they're always rushing to join a new order.

Since they never see their own shortcomings,
they're forever blaming their masters.

This is desire, brother; it's not love!
The lover has but one master of love.

Your constant changing of direction arises from desire,
not from love, O lost one!

It is desire that pulls to war and peace,
and is forever changing its hue.

This desire is now in concord, now in conflict,
now a friend, now a stranger.

Now it wants someone fervently;
now it has become a fierce enemy.

❖ ❖ ❖ ❖

If you were to give up your heart to a master on the path,
you would never detach your heart from that master.

All else that you give you can claim back,
but how can you reclaim the heart pledged to another?

To do so means that from the beginning you did not give your heart
but acted merely from desire.

Surrendering oneself means forgetting one's self;
the aim of Sufism is to become nothing.

If you surrender yourself and thus have no self,
then how can you go another way?

Open your eyes! This is the way of the valiant!
This is a matter of surrendering self and soul!

A man like Shams[2] can be found in any age,
but where is a Rumi to surrender his head?

There is many a Shams of Tabriz to be found,
but not everyone has a love like Rumi's.

The Shams of the time is not hidden from people,
but there's only one who can love him like Rumi.

❖ ❖ ❖ ❖

I spoke of love — pure love has three conditions:
the first is that one must possess a worthy, shining essence,

an essence that over the years
is cleansed of the stain of the passions.

One with a bad essence is far from love;
the eye that is blind can see no light.

The second condition is that one must be well-trained,
so as to be prepared from the very first day.

The third condition is that one must enjoy God's favor,
the special grace of that Absolute Friend,

Who sends His friends
to show the way to Him.

❖ ❖ ❖ ❖

Sufism is the crucible of hearts,
in which the genuine and the counterfeit within everybody come to light.

That which is bitter in nature emerges from the crucible as such;
that which is basically sweet comes out nectar-like.

The time it takes for the truth to emerge from the touchstone
varies with each person.

One's essence may be revealed in a month;
sometimes it may take a full forty years.

Most often it takes until old age
before the control of the mind is weakened,

when things are made easy for the carnal self
and its true nature is revealed.

This is why after the passage of years
a nature that's bitter is fully revealed.

❖ ❖ ❖ ❖

I spoke of love — that's different from desire.
Love has no "I" and "we"; love is being no one.

It is desire that makes you want to be a Sufi
so you may feel superior to others.

It is this desire that whispers in your ear,
"Be a master! Dominate those who are fools."

It is desire that urges, "Why doubt?
The only perfect mystic is you!

Consider others to be lacking and unworthy;
rally all the ignorant around you.

Gather those who are ruled by desire;
boast of your miracles and spiritual stations

so that, moved by desire, they praise your work
and lavish you with their souls and worldly goods."

Such sorcery is to provide contentment
for the cunning self.

This is why one is warned of the dangers of the path
and the provisions on the way are patience and endurance.

So, you should not go to just anyone,
for there are many monsters on this path.

Here God's hand must guide
and assist the people of heart.

God guides you step by step
so that you may not be waylaid by thieves.

❖ ❖ ❖ ❖

I spoke of love — its substance is sincerity,
which nurses the heart as if it were a child.

If you approach God with sincerity,
you won't run the risk of going astray.

Sincerity will distance you from the people of desire;
it will attract you towards and transform you into light.

Sincerity will show you the way of guidance
if you let it be your teacher on the path.

Sincerity with God and His creation
will make it easy for you to know the people of heart.

It will smooth your way to Unity
and transform your body into soul.

The seeker who travels the path with sincerity —
his soul is never inclined towards crookedness and deception.

Through sincerity he will find the One he seeks;
through sincerity he will surrender to his Beloved.

❖ ❖ ❖ ❖

I spoke of love — its place is the heart;
where there is no heart, loving becomes difficult.

Where there is no heart, love has no abode;
the only place for love is within the heart.

Where there is no heart, love cannot be found;
where there is no heart, love can't be revealed.

Where there is no heart, love can bear no fruit;
the lover's burning and endurance take place in the heart.

Acquire a heart, O wretched ones,
and your words and claims will take effect!

Acquire a heart, illuminate your soul,
and you'll be released from the darkness of "I" and "we."

Acquire a heart, become a human being;
then you will be privy to God's own mystery.

Whoever has no heart is no more than a corpse;
the dead-hearted one is unworthy of the Beloved.

Until you escape from the state of desire,
you'll never be in reach of a heart.

If you trample upon the image of "I" and "we,"
you'll find yourself living in the district of the heart.

Though deliverance from self is a difficult task,
if you accomplish that you'll have arrived at the first stage of the heart.

Drunkenly stamp upon your own being;
night and day consider yourself to have nothing,

so that you may receive God's grace
and come to possess a heart.

❖ ❖ ❖ ❖

We've arrived at the point of defining what a Sufi is —
in fact, a Sufi has no existence in the world.

A Sufi is someone who has been delivered from self
and has committed his heart to God.

In this entangling world a Sufi possesses
and desires nothing.

The Sufi is one who is empty of self;
he is unaware whether he exists or not.

One who becomes a Sufi is never truly a Sufi
until he is annihilated totally from himself.

As long as you are thinking in terms of possessing more or less,
how can you possibly be a Sufi, brother?

As long as you are still conscious of "I" and "we,"
how can you be secure from the deceit of your base self?

You go about talking like a Sufi
in order to hide your inward corruption

so that people won't realize what you really are,
what you are doing and what you desire.

In truth, you are putting a spell on yourself,
you're a slave of the self and thus your heart is distressed.

No one can become a Sufi by making outward claims;
you must have love in the heart and inward burning.

The Sufi path is one of *faqr* and *fana*,
free from all attachment and involvement in the world.

The Sufi is adorned with God's Attributes;
the Sufi's substance is the Essence of God.

If you don't suffer the pain of love, stay away!
Stay out of the circle of the people of heart.

Since you are not aware of their mysteries,
you will reject them out of suspicion.

This increases your darkness
and deprives you of humanity.

Don't play with the tails of the lions of God;
do not create havoc out of your ignorance!

❖ ❖ ❖ ❖

All in all, whatsoever I say is not love itself;
unless you have a heart you cannot know what love is.

Love requires a heart free from everything other than God
so that the light of Reality may burn brightly therein.

Love requires a heart that is like the clearest mirror,
that the Light Bestower of the soul might shine His light upon it.

LISTEN TO THE WINE

Listen to the wine as it tells a tale,
as it gives an account of the vat of Unity.

Whatever its color, wine is wine;
those drunk on wine know this.

Put aside the imaginary forms of color and aroma
so that you will see that all wines come from but one jug.

Attention to the color confuses you,
distracting you from the wine and the drinking of it.

❖ ❖ ❖

Drinking wine makes you drunk;
wine delivers you from self-existence.

How could the mere name "wine" ease your difficulties?
How could the cup without the wine put soul in your body?

The word "wine" is like an empty cup; it is not the same as real wine.
Wine worship is not a simple path and practice.

Wine must be drunk from the cup.
How can the word "wine" make one drunk?

Wine must be blended with the soul;
it does no good if poured down one's front!

You have slyly poured the wine inside your shirt;
you spend night and day talking about yourself.

You have not been aware that the adepts are present,
keeping an eye on you and your tricks.

They see your inner state in your eyes;
they pay no attention to your talk.

❖ ❖ ❖

Love of God pours wine in your goblet;
one cannot receive this gift by pretention.

Only when God wills can you become a wine drinker
and find your way to the sanctuary of the wine seller.

Only when the sunlight of God's love falls upon your roof
can you be fulfilled by the intoxication of this wine.

Only when God's hand seizes yours
can your soul become drunk with God.

The wine of God's love makes you drunk,
leaving you bereft of self-existence.

God's wine has nothing to do with Sufi caps and robes
or seeking out this or that Sufi order.

The mystery of love does not lie in begging-bowls and axes;[1]
one must be valiant to sacrifice one's soul for love.

Sufism is not a matter of hooting and shouting,
nor of lengthy scrolls with chains of spiritual lineage.

There must indeed be a chain — one of devotion — to capture the heart
so that the cry of the heart may reach the ear of the soul.

❖ ❖ ❖ ❖

When the heart is torn apart with love of God,
it comes to the path, eager and willing.

It seizes the hem of the cloak of a master of hearts
and finds a home in the district of loving-kindness.

When through drunkenness the Sufi loses his heart and self,
fidelity will bring him to God's path.

Unadulterated wine is poured into his cup,
and he drinks that wine of Unity.

Through drunkenness he passes beyond his own existence;
through annihilation of self he transcends self-existence.

He remains far from the transitory "I" and "we"[2]
and veiled from others in the realm of non-existence.

He becomes a stranger to the world of "we" and "you,"[3]
finally free from the need for the wine and the cup.

Now in union with God he has broken all bonds
and has offered up his soul to the Beloved, having chosen only Him.

LISTEN TO THE REED PLAYER

Listen to the mysteries of love from the Reed Player,
to the tale of love, full of burning and acceptance.

The melody of the reed is the tale of the Reed Player;
it is drunkenness and disgrace and the craziness of love.

It is the Reed Player's breath that brings forth the outcry of the reed;
His fire is ignited inside the reed.

Whatever the Reed Player recounts
the reed in turn relates by wailing.

Otherwise, the reed is but a piece of dry wood;
its cry is not from suffering or agitation.

❖ ❖ ❖ ❖

If your innermost ear hears its cry
you'll come to know why it wails.

It tells you, "If every part of me is resonating,
it is not from me; all sound, all strains are from Him.

For years I was a plain, leafless reed,
weak, luckless and uncreative.

Distant from Reality and caught up with appearances,
my soul was unaware of intimations and mysteries.

Finally, I gave my heart, gambled away my soul,
and separated myself from all involvement with the self.

I had been a weed, but when I came to know
His lips, I transformed into a reed.

I broke myself until union with Him welcomed me;
what seemed like defeat was for me, in fact, a victory.

Stripped of everything, I learned the lessons of love;
I attuned myself to His love until I was burnt up."

❖ ❖ ❖ ❖

"My heart was not bound to love's seven valleys;
that is why they call me the reed of seven segments.[1]

Once holes were scorched into my body,
His kiss brought forth from me a beautiful cry.

I was annihilated from self, then He breathed into me;
that breath created my fervor.

Love became my faith, creed and practice.
Humble lovers became my intimates.

My clamor is the cry of love and good fortune —
it comes from the breath of the Reed Player, not from my self."

❖ ❖ ❖ ❖

"Whoever comes to know the Beloved's love
will be rendered restless by my tune.

He will break into song on hearing my call;
he will feel love and ecstasy on hearing my cry.

My melody gladdens the depressed
and revives the lover whose heart has died.

If you become my confidant
your heart and soul may breathe with me."

❖ ❖ ❖ ❖

"If you hear my song you will be full of joy
and cease worrying about this and that.

I have no complaint about separation from the Beloved,
for I kiss Him madly on the lips!

How could a love-crazed lover ever complain
and tell the tale of his yearning for Him?

Love is not tied to spiritual station and state;
no sincere lover is attached to these things."

❖ ❖ ❖ ❖

"Who am I without His breath and His windpipe?
I am nothing; it is He Who is both reed player and reed.

Whoever is annihilated becomes lost in Him,
turning into the purest wine in the heart's vat.

My cry is the call of love and intimacy,
a joyful howl and a sorrow-free song.

Who am I to mention separation
or to sing about lack of provisions?

Without the Reed Player's lips I am silent;
this howl and this roar are from His breath.

I am content with whatever comes my way;
whatever happens to sting me is really a salve.

If you see me as a reed, it is only an appearance;
I do not exist; all being is but a single Being.

From the One Being comes all this clamor of mine,
this spirit-expanding melody and warmth.

I have gambled away everything, both my existence and non-existence,
so as to settle at the source and in union with Being.

Although I am the reed player, the reed and the reed's throat,
He is the cup, the cupbearer and the wine; I am nothing."

The reed has hundreds of discourses in its chest;
there are secrets and mysteries in the reed's song.

The reed's story is the refrain of being in love;
it tells of the way and the method of liberation.

Whoever loses self-existence becomes a reed
and, like wine, becomes altogether intoxicating.

❖ ❖ ❖ ❖

How long will you go on, Sufis, with your questioning?
Like a reed empty yourself of self

that you may be freed from the cloak of self-existence
and learn the mysteries of love.

Like the reed, on the feet of submission and contentment
pass out of the realm of "we" and "you."[2]

Shorn of heart and faith, like the love-crazed reed,
let out the cry of the heart at the feet of the Beloved.

Fervor and drunkenness are our method and faith;
the practice of love is our age-old creed.

LISTEN TO THE MASTER

Hear me now, that I may tell you who the master is,
though he is not involved in the commotion of existence.

Who is the master? That mystic who has lost his self,
who has no faith or religion other than God.

Who is the master? The one who separates you from self,
who empties you of self and fills you with God.

Who is the master? That traveler on God's way,
that guide on the path who knows pain.

Who is the master? The one who, in his innermost consciousness,
became nothing, for it is God Who is hidden within him.

Who is the master? The one who is
completely effaced and annihilated in God.

Who is the master? The one who, in remembering God,
is liberated from remembrance of all else.

Who is the master? The visible mirror of the Beloved,
within whose breast is only passion for Him.

Who is the master? One who has become a master through God,
who has been caught by the lasso of God's love.

The master is one who is free from self,
whose heart's hand grips tightly the hem of God's cloak.

❖ ❖ ❖ ❖

The master is the master of love, ecstasy and spiritual states;
he is not a master because of the passage of time.

He is a selfless *rend* who has burned away his own self-existence;
the eye of his soul is illuminated by the Beloved.

He is as humble as earth and as flowing as water;
he bestows light like the sun.

Though he exists within the realm of being,
in God's inner sanctuary he has no existence.

With one glance he can tell who you really are
and whether you are truly an intoxicated lover.

Does your soul have the aptitude to burn and endure,
or are you bound to the world of desire?

God's representative does not need to exaggerate
or boast, nor is he dependent on money or gifts.

Although ashamed of his own existence,
he is God's servant here, performing God's will.

He claims no visions or miraculous powers,
nor does he need to talk constantly about himself.

He has no trace in the world, nor does he exist,
though he is the spirit of the spirit and the soul of the soul.

He manifests God, as a theophany of Divine Oneness;
he is far from existence and multiplicity.

He has eaten the honey of contemplative vision from God's hive;
he is liberated from possessing more or less and from what is or what is not.

To him anything other than God is not worth a penny;
he is separated from everything, including himself.

Such a master is the guide on the way to Oneness;
it is appropriate to throw your head at his feet.

❖ ❖ ❖ ❖

Now listen, that I may speak more
about a particular group of wicked, so-called masters.

They are claimants trapped in the lasso of the ego,
who falsely declare themselves to be spiritual masters.

These would-be masters welcome one and all to their feast,
only to ensure that their own food is provided thereby.

Day and night they display their self-existence;
without having drunk spiritual wine they pretend to be intoxicated.

They claim to be masters and to guide others,
though they have not been guided by a master themselves.

O brother, open the eye of your heart!
Clear your circle of these deceitful people!

Do not listen to the talk of this base and morally bankrupt lot;
do not step into the world of fortune-tellers!

They will play all sorts of tricks on you;
ensnaring you in the web of the ego, they will make you sick.

When you become aware, it will be too late;
you will have nothing but a lost heart.

You will have lost wealth, a lifetime, and your soul;
moreover, you will have strayed far from the path.

These so-called masters, who claim to be sages,
have gone astray and are ignorant and cruel.

They follow their own egos and seek material profit;
they are out to rob the simple-hearted.

They claim to know love, yet merely talk about it;
their talk is nonsense because of their ignorance.

They insist on calling themselves Sufis,
but they are only concerned with misleading others.

Their attendants, tricky and gossipy,
buzz around them night and day.

They boast of miraculous and healing powers,
yet they even disparage Jesus.

Their claims are no more than empty talk;
their intentions are to gain status and wealth.

❖ ❖ ❖ ❖

I have been told how a truly selfless master
set out once with a charlatan Sufi.

The latter gradually became closer to the master
and told him more and more of his secrets.

Murderer, criminal and power-seeker,
he had held a high position in his own land.

He'd had a master who had died, and
so was stranded on the path without a guide.

The master asked, "Why did you wander off?
Why did you abandon that order?"

He answered, "My heart became confused and
could not help me; it did not accept his successor.

That master had no power or spiritual intoxication.
Why should I serve one who is powerless?"

At this, the master told him, "Serve a worldly leader;
have nothing further to do with the spiritual path.

You are only concerned with power and wealth and talk;
in a state like this do not complain of having no master!

Crows are made to flock together with crows;
the nightingale converses just with the rose."

❖ ❖ ❖ ❖

Now I'll disclose another secret;
open the ear of the soul to learn.

People tend to worship idols;
with heart and soul, passionately they adore idols.

Such idol-worshiping people
seek idols everywhere.

In fact, these people are really worshiping their own nature;
they are the followers of the mirror's reflection of their own face.

Although they claim to have many masters,
they are captivated by their own desire.

❖ ❖ ❖ ❖

If you have a breast that is burning,
do not entrust your heart to a counterfeit master.

Seek God within yourself; a selfless master
is not concerned with self-promotion.

Love cannot be practiced by brokers;
the lover of God does not follow an imposter.

THE SILENCE AND *ADAB* OF THE SUFIS

Listen, O Sufis, to this discourse on our inner state
so that your souls may become free of idle talk.

Talk is not appropriate in the company of the drunken;
silence is golden for the Sufi who is pure.

By silence we do not mean the closing of one's lips;
we mean containing oneself while burning.

Many a Sufi sits in silence
while his heart stirs within his breast.

Though his lips are closed to speech,
speech abounds in the Sufi's eyes.

Many a Sufi who speaks fine words with eloquence
does not have a burning heart and an anguished soul.

One must become silent both outwardly and inwardly,
without thought of fire and light or sting and salve,

for the Sufi's state is higher than these;
the devotee of the Truth is beyond such experiences.

Progress on the path is not measured by clamor and commotion;
the Sufi's fervor and inner state are governed by the heart.

If a Sufi lets go of himself
words become worthless to him.

Observing true silence, in reality he has no existence;
that silence is the mystery, the secret, of drunkenness.

A spiritual state itself is no better than talk to him;
people of heart are not concerned with states.

He is liberated from spiritual states and stations;
he is not a seeker of the miraculous.

Since his God-seeking is without limit,
he is totally obliterated in God and does not exist.

❖ ❖ ❖ ❖

If you consider yourself a Sufi,
why are you so attached to words?

The heart uses another language;
the speech of the heart communicates in a different way.

The heart's discourse is not in words;
its realm is above that of "I" and "we."[1]

People of the heart speak with one tongue,
though the words and phrases are innumerable.

Become acquainted with the vision of the people of heart
so that you may learn the secrets of love.

❖ ❖ ❖ ❖

The Sufi breaks free from all limits and bonds;
he surrenders completely, both outwardly and inwardly.

O Sufi, abandon the observance of *adab*;
the people of heart are beyond mere manners.

While you are traveling the path you must observe *adab*,
but when you reach God your *adab* will be considered unbelief.

Reason says, "Mind your manners!"
Love declares, "Break free from your self!"

While you are thinking about *adab*, you are governed by reason;
you are dragging your feet in the practice of love.

One who is annihilated in God transcends *adab*
and closes the book of etiquette.

Give up *adab* and follow your heart;
be drunk and love-crazed in pursuit of the Beloved!

To show off your *adab* is an expression of self-existence;
the convention of lovers is intoxication.

As long as you focus on manners you make a display of your self,
a focus and display that distance you from Being Itself.

Become crazy on the path of loving!
Become estranged from yourself and your world.

If you come to dwell in God's sanctuary,
you'll become free from fear and hope.

You'll be free from existence and its ups and downs;
its joy, pain and sorrow will all be the same.

Be a person of heart and therefore without self!
Be a mad lover! Be a dervish!

As long as you are concerned with outward *adab*,
you will not discover the mysteries of the heart's inner sanctuary.

❖ ❖ ❖ ❖

Leave behind manners, words and talk,
station and state, ecstasy and shouting.

If you seek the Beloved, stay silent;
let your outward and inward being become an ear.

Whoever opens the heart's eye to God
becomes free from all *adab* and discussion.

One is concerned with neither spiritual state nor speech;
one has no question, no "why" in one's mind.

One gives up both worlds, becoming annihilated,
free of concern for what is proper *adab*.

While you talk of your identity and your reputation
you are occupied with loving yourself.

As long as you are a prisoner of self, preoccupied with spiritual states,
your place is secure at the "station" of mere talk.

❖ ❖ ❖ ❖

The Sufi who is sincere is stupefied and drunk,
unaware of everything except the Beloved.

He is in the tavern of ruin, lost from self,
like a grape that has become wine in the vat.

He is liberated from spiritual states, stations and shouting;
in reality, he is no one other than the Friend.

Otherwise, he is a Sufi only in name,
a title for impressing others.

How long will you remain trapped in the bonds of words?
If you call yourself a Sufi, you must die to your self.

How long are you going to remain in the cage?
Open the door! Be drunk! Be crazy! Take flight!

Otherwise, my friend, you're no Sufi. Be gone!
Don't bother to look for the home of the Simorgh.[2]

To reach the Mount Qaf[3] of nothingness,
dispense with "I am this, you are that."

Spur your heart on, like Rakhsh,[4] racing towards God,
until He bestows light upon your annihilation.

LOVE AND DESIRE

A disciple who had fallen behind on the path appealed
with sighs and inner pain to a master whose heart was aware:

"What is love and what is the love story?" he asked. "Which is
the right path, and who is the true traveler on the path of love?

Vague and cryptic discourses on this subject abound,
but none is illuminating or provides an answer to my problem.

No one has disclosed the secrets of love
or the part desire plays in the venture of love.

Reveal the truth about the heart and love;
address and expound on the role of desire."

❖ ❖ ❖ ❖

To this, his master replied with these words,
lifting the veil from the mystery:

"The source of God's creation was love; it was by means
of love that God's breath bestowed life to all.[1]

Love's work involves many stages,
which not all are fit to attain.

In the beginning desire had a share in love;
it was a stream in the realm of the heart.

Desire is like a river, and love is
the ocean that most rivers seek.

Many of these, however, dry up
in the desert before reaching the ocean.

Many kinds of love are merely carnal desires;
however beautiful, they are no more than games.

Though desire may lead to love's shore,
it has no access to the ocean's inner depths.

Desire is lust, chatter and flirtation; it is
only an expression of the self in its neediness.

Desire arises from one's instinct and has
many hundreds of ordinary modes of expression."

❖ ❖ ❖ ❖

"Desire is sometimes like the behavior of a donkey;
bestial lust is its most primitive expression.

One who becomes as base and crude as a donkey
is transformed into a creature of obsessive lust.

Sometimes the deceiving, lustful person
becomes fanatically opposed to any rival.

He becomes like a self-righteous rooster,
unrivaled in voicing its desire.

He does not use force like the donkey,
for he is not blinded by lust.

He is playful and mischievous, with coquettish airs,
like the rooster displaying its plumes in lustful desire.

When this desire embraces flirtation
and affection, it may satisfy carnal love."

❖ ❖ ❖ ❖

"There are many kinds of worldly love;
most are forms of verbal persuasion and games of passion.

One example is the approach of the nightingale,
who seems to dote on the rose.

Its practice of loving is neither sincere nor pure;
its love is neither affectionate nor loyal.

Night and day it warbles plaintive appeals,
broadcasting its secret everywhere.

The *rendan* pay no attention to its moans when
it makes a clamor due to separation from the rose.

All its ranting and raving are immature conduct,
which true lovers consider a disgrace.

The rose is wary of the frenzied nightingale,
for no fidelity exists in its brand of love.

Wherever roses bloom, the nightingale
turns its heart and gazes in their direction.

It perches near a rose flirtatiously, while sharing
secrets and showing interest in another bloom.

Then at dawn it becomes the lover of the narcissus,
wooing it with amorous glances and declarations.

Yet again, it loses interest and flies away
from there and pines for another flower.

Since no real burning and acceptance reside
in its breast, its mournful cries are just a ruse.

This is a carnal and futile love, for the nightingale
seeks nothing but the hue and scent of the rose."

❖ ❖ ❖ ❖

"The rose's love is carnal as well,
for it has no passion or depth.

The rose seeks a playful lover;
the zephyr is unaware of the rose's plot,

so the rose uses its color and sweet
scent to draw the zephyr near.

It shows its face with grace and coquetry,
while rank desire is hidden beneath its petals.

Once the zephyr is aroused and loses control,
the rose tries to capture it through a hundred different ruses

so that the zephyr will become crazed with desire
and head for the garden to find union."

❖ ❖ ❖ ❖

"These sensual games of lovers, however,
are not all there is to love.

The zephyr sets the rose's heart aflutter,
rendering it frenzied and restless.

It, too, is full of doubt and hypocrisy,
for such love is guided by mere desire.

Without this desire, there would be no flirtation;
the zephyr would not drift toward roses.

If the lover tears his garment to express longing,
he is only showing off in love's marketplace.

This clamor and crying are merely trickery and deception,
for true love has no hunter, prey or snare.

In the eyes of the *rendan*, the love enjoyed by
the rose and zephyr is mere desire and has no worth."

❖ ❖ ❖ ❖

"Yet another form of love is the commotion of the moth,
who is said to be captivated and crazed by the candle.

As soon as the moth spies the candle's flame,
it darts towards it from every corner.

It hurls itself upon the flame till it dies,
delivering its heart and sweet soul to this beloved.

Such love, too, is not a pure love;
it is only by deception that this love shines.

When the moth offers its soul to its beloved in the flame,
it is showing off with this display of fireworks.

Then at dawn with the fervor it once had for the flame,
the moth takes flight towards the garden.

It is neither faithful to one beloved nor love-crazed at all,
for it becomes drunk in the garden as well.

Its object of love is the rose by day,
and it burns with love for the candle's flame by night.

In the realm of the real lovers this is not true love,
for love allows no pretense or self-display."

❖ ❖ ❖ ❖

"The candle expresses yet another form of love,
its head being consumed by love's passion.

It appears to be a sincere and God-seeking lover
that burns with a feverish fire.

But this love's zeal comes from its head;
the candle spends a lifetime in thought.

The candle's passion is all in its head;
below, its heart is cold and depressed.

Openly its head blazes brightly,
but its heart, hidden away, is not radiant.

Its love is like that of the philosopher,
who seeks the eternal by reason's light.

He does not know that it is the heart's fire,
not the fervor in his head, that is both guide and way.

The path is traversed through the heart's love.
What use is life if it is just burnt away?"

❖ ❖ ❖ ❖

"Another example of this kind of artful deception
is the refined love between man and woman.

In this love, the lover yearns with a heart
committed passionately to the beloved.

All the lover's hopes and thoughts are concerned with union;
such a lover thinks of nothing but the beloved.

But this love is transitory;
no one will find rest in such a love.

Once the loved one is dead and buried,
sighing and moaning are of no use.

However lofty this love may be,
it is not worthy of a love-crazed *rend*."

❖ ❖ ❖ ❖

"Though there are many cases of worldly love,
all are no more than desire; they are not true love.

Yet they can serve to fashion a ladder,
leading to the heart and its engagement in true love.

Suffering the pains of carnal love
may serve as the means to purify one's love.

When the lover flees the trap of desire,
he is unmatched in the realm of the heart.

He surmounts in one moment all the hurdles and trials,
and reaches the station of those with committed hearts.

In a divine manner, the lover merges with God
and drunkenly inspires the whole world.

He becomes a sincere lover, totally consumed by love
in the realm of drunkards with illuminated hearts.

All this is admissible and fair by love's decree,
but only if the heart is drunk and love-crazed.

True love is unlike carnal love;
it is utterly free of deception, need or greedy desire.

Love is true when self-existence is no more,
when all is fervor, intoxication and the craziness of love.

If you arrive in the world of the heart,
your soul will learn of the Sufi's love.

You'll learn that this love is higher than all the others,
being based upon direct perception and conviction.

The Sufi does not trill like the nightingale;
his pain is concealed in his heart and not expressed.

He does not hop from branch to branch,
but spends his life prostrate before one prayer niche.

He is not attached to color and scent like the rose,
for colorlessness is his own color.

He is not a show-off like the moth,
for the Sufi is not concerned with anyone but the Beloved.

His fervor is not in his head like that of the candle;
his heart is aflame, and his soul is burning.

The heart of the Sufi is consigned solely to the One
by whom many are stupefied and bewildered.

Though he has no knowledge of the Essence of God,
his heart is drunk with the wine of God's Attributes.

He is happy with God's grace and wrath;
he is content while inside the fire.

He wants from God neither this world nor the hereafter;
with Him, the Sufi has no need for words.

Since the Beloved is eternal and immortal,
the Sufi's love increases every day.

Such a Sufi is detached from self and both worlds
and is attached to God alone.

He becomes acquainted with his Lord,
Who becomes the Sufi's guide towards Himself."

THE HONEYBEE AND THE BLOSSOM

In the flower garden the honeybee said,
"I seek blossoms everywhere.

Whenever I find a fragrant blossom,
I take flight and head directly towards it.

When I find a yearning blossom that has torn open its chest,
I purify that chest from color and scent.

I make a home in the heart of that blossom;
I erect there a house built of love.

Not every blossom is worthy of gambling all for love;
I seek one that is free from "I" and "we."[1]

I seek a blossom that is not impure,
one whose heart is restless with yearning.

I want a blossom that will, with warm embrace,
welcome my sting as a salve.

I want a selfless blossom
that will not feel hurt by my sting.

I want an unquestioning blossom
that will surrender with love and purity.

I want a blossom that will, out of love and fidelity,
give up its existence and become annihilated in me.

I want a blossom that will bow its head at my feet
and place all that it has in my hands.

I want a blossom that will not think of what was
and will forget itself, self-interest and profit.

I want a blossom that has the pain of love
and will gamble its life in the backgammon of love."

❖ ❖ ❖ ❖

"For the rose, the pain of love is its fragrant aroma;
it expands the soul, bestows spirit and attracts the heart.

I sense the aromas on every side;
I seek them out in every direction.

I am repulsed by unpleasant odors;
only a horsefly is at home with foul smells.

How could the scents of the passions attract me?
My sting is not like that of the horsefly!

No sooner does the smell of hypocrisy meet my nostrils
than I rush to free myself from its presence.

How could my sting penetrate every thorny bramble?
How could a horsefly have an intuitive heart?

All that's bitter is sweetened by my sting,
while all is poisoned by the horsefly.

Though it may claim to effect a cure,
everyone knows what the horsefly is like.

You can find horseflies in numbers everywhere;
they have nothing to offer but what is most vile.

As soon as a horsefly enters a market,
its craving leads it straight to a carcass."

❖ ❖ ❖ ❖

"I am a customer for the perfume of blossoms;
I am the one who makes this trade flourish.

Wherever there's a blossom with a burning heart
I free it from the bonds of its physical form.

I make it drunk; I intoxicate it;
in fidelity I sting it to provide a cure.

My sting is always accompanied by its remedy;
fervor and passion go along with my cure.

My wrath's sting becomes healing balm;
my loving salve becomes fragrant honey.

The aroma of the rose draws me towards it,
so it can become fine honey by the grace of my sting.

My sting is obvious and my cure concealed;
the cure is the hidden meaning of my sting.

The sting of the needle transmits the healing cure;
the surgeon's lancet brings life to the ailing patient."

❖ ❖ ❖ ❖

Who is the honeybee? What does it symbolize?
Open the eye of the heart — it is none other than the master.

His sting and salve will gladden your heart
until the voice of your empty claims is silenced.

His cure and sting are affection and rebuff,
the alchemy by which you are transformed.

❖ ❖ ❖ ❖

Who is the blossom? The wayfarer on a straight path
who has submitted his heart to the guiding master.

He receives wholeheartedly the master's grace and wrath;
whatever the master wants he resolves to do.

He gives up his soul to the sword of the master's sting.
With a smile he delivers his soul to the Beloved.

With his heart he submits to that Beloved,
to be blown away by the wind of *fana*.

If you do not have the scent of love, keep your distance;
keep away from the precincts of the people of heart.

❖ ❖ ❖ ❖

The horsefly is that self-worshiping braggart
from whose poisonous breath people are not safe.

Outwardly he claims to be a Bayazid,[2]
while Shemr and Yazid[3] would feel ashamed of his true nature.

Stay away from him, for he'll make you ill;
his poison will make you feel disgusted with love.

Don't make the horsefly your object of adoration;
go and distinguish reality from illusion.

Bind your heart to one who is selfless;
kiss the dust on the path of the Sufi.

THE REMEMBRANCE OF GOD

The singer began a rapturous song;
my heart became enthralled and intoxicated.

Thus it was moved to explain some matters
in order to close down the shops of those who profit from Sufism.

It speaks of the mystery and spiritual experience of *zekr*,
so that some people will not become dealers thereof.

O Sufi! You who claim to remember God,
your every breath is dedicated to an idol.

You call out to God, while being heedless of Him;
you talk of water, while you stand on the shore.

You perform remembrance of God just to worship yourself;
night and day you make a display of your own existence.

You call out to God through *zekr* in such a way
that each moment you are merely calling yourself to mind.

When your ego draws you into unbelief,
you turn to prayers and *zekr*.

What *zekr* is this, that increases your self-existence
and brings you into sobriety from intoxication!

What *zekr* is this, that distances you from Divine Unity
and makes you the hireling of your deceitful self!

What *zekr* is this, that leads you to plunge into the maelstrom of carnal self
through your devilish nature!

What *zekr* is this, that through the self and its desires
consumes you with hope of gaining food and possessions!

What *zekr* is this, that releases your lusts
like a thief disguised as a guard!

What *zekr* is this, with which you still exist,
where you are not yet delivered from the self!

What *zekr* is this, in which self-existence persists and where
lust is the beloved and craving the cupbearer!

What *zekr* is this, that has increased your self-conceit and through which,
rather than becoming free, you have imprisoned yourself!

❖ ❖ ❖ ❖

Real *zekr* is a matter for the heart;
it is not a matter for the flesh.

Real *zekr* takes place when you have heart-consciousness
and are not self-worshiping and futile.

Real *zekr* is that which takes over your breath,
not that which arises from the windpipe of desire.

Real *zekr* is that which burns up your soul,
not that which teaches the cult of self-conceit.

Real *zekr* is that which makes you drunk
and releases you from all thought of being.

Real *zekr* is that which takes away what you have
and fills up your whole being with itself

in such a way that nothing remains of you
and you can no longer discern yourself.

Real *zekr* occurs when only the Remembered One remains,
when the heart forgets the rememberer and remembering.

❖ ❖ ❖ ❖

It is *zekr* when you no longer exist.
If God exists eternally, who are you to imagine you exist?

Zekr is that which takes you from yourself,
which calls you away from self-existence to non-existence.

It is *zekr* if you have repented from identity, and, absent from self,
have turned your attention towards God alone.

Zekr means deliverance from "we" and "I"[1]
and arrival at the station of security.

It is *zekr* if it makes you unable to distinguish
others from yourself, and good from bad.

❖ ❖ ❖ ❖

If your *zekr* is just a name made up of letters,
an audio tape will repeat the name better than you.

A tape that is recorded with the name of God
can run night and day without showing off.

Yet even if this tape were to run for years,
it could not attain the quality of a human being.

You practice *zekr*, but you are far from its meaning;
the masters of heart consider you to be no more than a tape.

Zekr is a name, seek the Named;
zekr is like form, seek content.

The name will carry you to the Named,
from the realm of form to that of content.

Only by way of drunkenness and becoming nothing
will you become released from self and attain the Named.

For us the name represents a Name and Attribute of God,
which makes your heart increase in gnosis.

For us mere utterance represents just the form of the word;
the form of the word never opened the way for anyone.

If your *zekr* only involves the form of the word,
its result is trickery and deception.

If you realize even one of the Names of God,
you will shed the limited and become the Absolute.

Seek to open the treasure of the Named with the key of a Name;
otherwise you will never be able to break this spell.

If you practice *zekr* and still have self-existence,
be aware, O brother, that you are still an idol-worshiper.

Believe me, you are secretly worshiping idols
with your various prayers and your silent *zekr*.

You are worshiping idols in the name of God;
you drink vinegar and play drunk to impress people.

Outwardly you have attached yourself to God,
inwardly you have become attached to your self.

This way you have things upside down:
you affirm yourself while denying God!

You claim to have powers and visions,
but your whole being is tainted by your carnal self.

You satisfy your passions with fantasies
by telling stories about the past.

Don't reduce real love to that which is false;
Don't play around with the tail of the Lion!

❖ ❖ ❖ ❖

Outwardly you claim to be Bayazid;[2]
inwardly you are wicked and in the clutches of your carnal self.

Outwardly you have become a master free of passions;
inwardly you buzz with the instincts of a horsefly.

Your aim is not to initiate others into *zekr*,
but rather to pass on your ego to them.

A group of vulgar people, all followers of desire,
worship you with deceit and pretension.

Birds of your feather will flock to you
and fall at your feet crying in humility.

They have found an egotistical pharaoh with whom they can identify;
they have discovered in you the manifestation of their own true nature.

As a result, your ego is joyful,
for truth, too, was trampled by you.

❖ ❖ ❖ ❖

You are not worthy of *zekr*, do not make light of it;
God honors those who are truly engaged in its practice.

You worship yourself — what have you got to do with God?
You are unfaithful — how then can you care about purity?

If you are not selfless, you cannot truly practice *zekr*,
for someone who merely mouths *zekr* is not a Sufi.

The heart of one moved by desire cannot be engaged in *zekr*;
its utterance merely increases hypocrisy.

If you practice *zekr*, forget yourself;
with *zekr* you have to shed the foundation of your self-existence.

❖ ❖ ❖ ❖

If you are ready to practice *zekr*
and to be purged of self-consciousness,

then go and repent of the sin of your self-existence;
and drunkenly stamp out everything else!

With the blade of neediness cut off the head of your coyness;
grab the hem of the cloak of one who provides the cure,

so that out of loving-kindness he may glance towards you
and pour the wine of non-existence into your jug,

LISTEN TO THE CUPBEARER

Listen to the cupbearer, who is making a commotion,
exposing the fake drunkards.

He says, "These people who are acting drunk
are in fact displaying self-existence.

Their crying out like Sufis is really the yell of the self and lust;
it is from neither burning of the soul nor pain for God.

They're drunk with the wine of arrogance and pride;
they're far from the vat and the wine cellar of love."

❖ ❖ ❖ ❖

"I will never pour wine in just any cup.
My wine is not just water flowing in a ditch.

I will pour wine only into the cup
of one whose nature is primed.

He must first offer up his being to me,
for that is the price of a drop of my wine.

By giving him my purest wine
I will separate him from his ego.

Intoxication from my cup takes one away from self;
one's drunkenness will never wane, as it is eternal."

❖ ❖ ❖ ❖

"Now let me tell you of a group of imposters
who deceitfully call themselves 'masters.'

They all scheme to swindle people;
they are void of purity and truth.

They are slaves to the ego and desire;
they 'guide' people with their trickery and antics.

They are drunk with the wine of selfishness and pride;
they are talented experts in fooling people.

Their cups are empty of the wine of true meaning;
all of their claims derive from rank stupidity."

❖ ❖ ❖ ❖

"They speak of transcendence with the roll of drums;
their adherents are an ignorant pack of sycophants.

They may consider themselves to be like Bayazid;[1]
inwardly, however, they are like Yazid.[2]

People who are filled with selfish desire follow them,
being well aware of their tricks and deceit.

They gather around them for the sake of status and wealth,
telling tall tales about their working wonders and their spiritual states.

They talk about miracles and spiritual stations;
they are out to trick innocent people.

They use thousands of schemes to gather
ordinary people into their snares.

These imposters are in the grip of lust;
they are paragons of negligence, ignorance and deception."

❖ ❖ ❖ ❖

"Indeed, these men, who still exist, are not drunk with wine;
they lie in wait for simple, naive people.

My wine is not an intoxicant meant for monsters;
the feast of Divine Unity is not for befuddled fools.

The basis of Divine Unity is drunkenness and selflessness;
being nothing is the essence of being a Sufi.

The Sufis have the way and practice of the friends of God,
renouncing consciousness of self and boastful claims."

❖ ❖ ❖ ❖

"The one who makes a show of doing prayers
is not drunk with love but is just a trickster.

Though he may do exegesis of the Qur'an,
in reality he is just brainwashing the ignorant.

If his table is laden with food and drink,
it is because his hands are in the pockets of other people."

❖ ❖ ❖ ❖

"Another one claims to be a healer,
but in reality his vocation is to destroy.

He boasts about healing the blind and lame;
however, he is just spouting gibberish and empty words.

While being sick himself he wants to treat others,
making people ill in body and soul."

❖ ❖ ❖ ❖

"Another discloses openly so-called secrets,
though these 'mysteries' do not come from the Divine Essence.

He is confirmed as a man of insights and a discerner of mysteries,
but only by his carnal self.

And, being ignorant of the tricks of the base ego,
the idiot calls himself 'master of all arts.'"

❖ ❖ ❖ ❖

"Another considers himself a saint
and mesmerizes people by chanting God's names.

He makes a Sufi-seeming clamor before the ignorant
but only leads people further from God.

This chanting is just for making a living,
as if to say, 'O people, I am short of funds!'"

❖ ❖ ❖ ❖

Another dreams and tells fortunes
and rolls his head about to feign ecstasy,

claiming, 'I'm a perfect human being;
there's no master like me in this day and age.'"

❖ ❖ ❖ ❖

"Another dresses in white
to hide the tarnish over his heart.

He wears a white robe just to show off,
to make others fall into his trap.

He doesn't know that the heart's work is not about showing off;
the dress of the friends of God is the color of colorlessness."

❖ ❖ ❖ ❖

"Another fills many pages, delivering verbose accounts
about 'the school of God's gnosis,'

all to satisfy his own cunning self, which is
the source of all his words.

His aim is to make ignorant people
throw silver and gold at his feet."

❖ ❖ ❖ ❖

"Another type of charlatan is one
who uses obscure discourse as his trap,

Fortifying himself with drugs to smoke,
he uses them to manipulate the simpleminded.

He uses hallucinogens to drag them to the stars,
for which the toll exacted is their souls and all they own.

He makes claims about his own achievements,
but his so-called miracles are made by hashish and hemp."

❖ ❖ ❖ ❖

"Another, to engage in discourse on mysticism,
first grows a special kind of moustache,

believing that whoever does not sport twisted whiskers
will not be able to serve as a guide on the path.

He wears his hair long like a woman,
claiming, 'I am the perfect Sufi of the time,

and no one is allowed to follow the Sufi path
without a moustache and long hair!'"

❖ ❖ ❖ ❖

"Yet another one talks loudly about the sharia
and only mentions the spiritual path in secret.

He is full of airs and self-importance
and is obviously proud of his religion and dogmas.

To save himself from the muftis' anathema
he does whatever they demand.

He is a slave to the world, as everyone can see,
even though he constantly claims to transcend it.

All this he does to make himself acceptable in other people's eyes
and thereby remain safe from the sting of their reproach.

This trickster is drunk with pretense;
his aim is to lead astray a group of clueless people."

❖ ❖ ❖ ❖

"The fact is that these sober pretenders are not drunk,
even though they call themselves 'drunkards.'

These base people have not offered up their hearts;
they have not drunk the wine from the vat of Unity.

All of them are ignorant of divine love;
they are fervently drunk on their own self-existence.

Their jugs contain no genuine red wine;
their fake wine is nothing but colored water.

They poison cup after cup
with countless tricks and fairy tales.

The cup of these self-worshiping charlatans
is full of deceit and superstition.

Even though they do it in the name of Sufism,
all their trickery and posturing

is not the way of God; it is not Sufism.
O brother, you must value your love!

Drunkenness from God is far from deception;
fulfilling human potential is our creed and practice.

Drunkenness from our wine brings peace and purity,
the essence of which is love and fidelity.

It is love's religion sanctioned by God;
this teaching will last forever."

THE PRAYER OF *SAMA*

O Lord, we have no friend other than You,
we find no solace except in Your refuge.

You know the secrets of each and every Sufi;
You alone can solve all their problems.

O Lord, grant us an intellect that seeks only You
and a tongue that speaks only Your name.

O Lord, grant us a heart that longs for nearness to You
and that contains no desire but the desire for You.

O Lord, You know what we truly want!
Bestow whatever You wish, as You can do as You please.

Grant purity to hearts that are enraptured with You;
bestow sustenance on the destitute of Your lane.

May You gladden all hearts with intoxication,
so they find release from the bonds of self-existence.

نی نامه‌ها

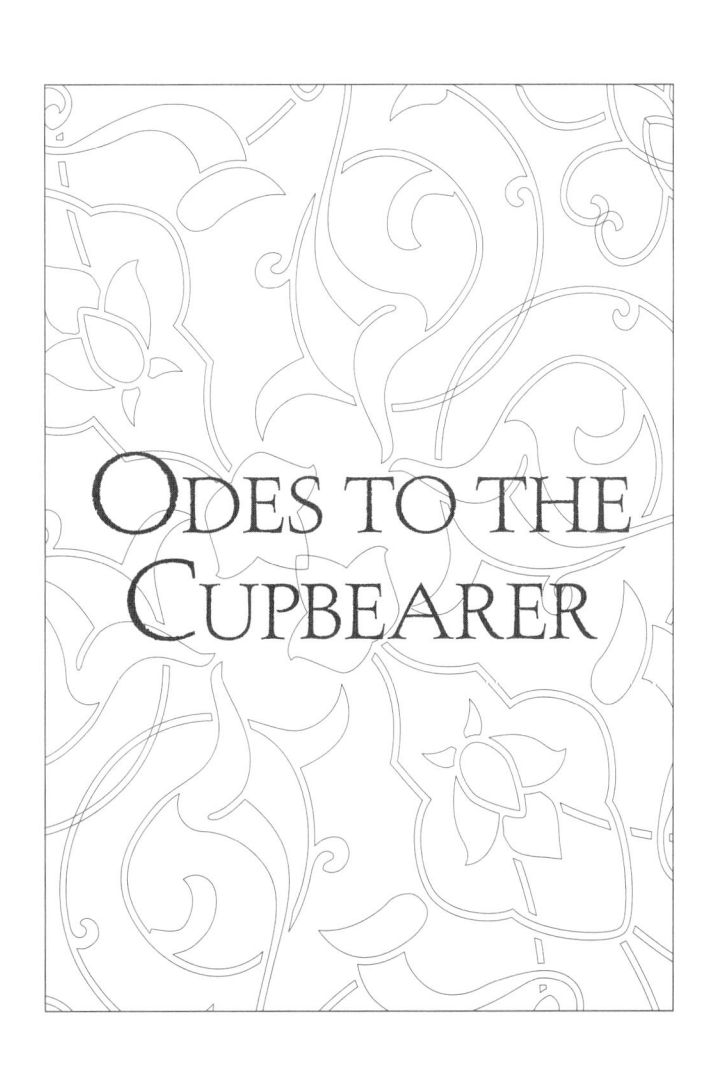

Odes to the Cupbearer

ODE TO THE CUPBEARER 1[1]

Give me the wine, cupbearer, that burns my soul,
that burns away all worries about this and that.

Give me a fire that melts me down,
then evaporates the water and annihilates my existence.

Give me a wine that makes me lost from myself,
that I might shatter the jug and submerge myself in the vat.

Give me a wine that sets my soul ablaze,
that burns away my heart and soul as well as all thought.

Give me a wine that makes me drunk,
that sets me free from the darkness of self-existence.

Give me a wine that drives me mad,
that turns me into a stranger to all creation.

Give me a wine that relieves me of self,
that I might dwell safely in a corner of the tavern.

Let the tavern of Unity become my home,
so that my heart desires and beholds nothing but God.

ODE TO THE CUPBEARER 2 [1]

O cupbearer, bring me a goblet of wine,
for I have fallen far from wisdom's way!

I am bewildered, restless, wandering;
I am a hung-over drunk at your feet.

My heart has neither patience nor rest;
I have no strength to escape or flee.

The companions have gone; I have fallen behind.
Give me wine for I am weary of both body and soul.

Give me wine that sets fire to the soul
and drives from the mind the thought of this and that;

Wine that burns away my whole being
and frees me from worries about everything;

Wine that makes me forget
and separates me from my self;

Wine that melts away my being
and takes me in drunkenness far from self;

Wine that carries me towards *fana*,
that takes me on the path that God desires;

Wine that polishes the heart of its sorrow
and liberates me from thoughts of having more or less;

Wine that makes me weep tears like the candle,
that burns me so fully that, like the candle, I will not rise again;

Wine that prevents my heart from crying out,
that makes me burn like the moth and be silent;

Wine that takes me from my self
so that I will be accepted by the Beloved;

Wine that eases all my difficulty
and liberates me from the bonds of physical existence;

Wine that Your *rendan* drink,
that keeps them intoxicated and bewildered by you;

Wine that nourishes the elect
and increases sincerity every moment.

Through philosophy, the mystery of the universe was never revealed,
nor has anyone ever found the secret of this bowl of dust.

For the intellect's currency we found to be of no use;
may wine then cure our pain!

ODE TO THE CUPBEARER 3 [1]

O cupbearer, start bestowing your favor.
Open the wine house once again!

A gust of self-existence got caught in my throat;
idol-worship has seized my being.

The noise of multiplicity has disturbed my peace,
robbed me of strength and left me weary of life.

Please open wide the door so that
my heart may soar off to the wine house!

Let me flee from the world of "I" and "we," [2]
and let me set foot in the valley of safety.

❖ ❖ ❖ ❖

O cupbearer, give me water that has a fiery nature,
for the currency of self-existence has no worth.

Cupbearer, give me that problem-solving wine,
to distinguish reality from imagination.

Cupbearer, give me that wine that burns my soul,
teaching me the path of selflessness.

Cupbearer, give me that wine that will make me silent,
and wrap me in the cloak of nothingness.

Cupbearer, give me that wine that drowns my self-esteem
and carries me beyond all thought of right and wrong.

Cupbearer, give me that wine, that I might lose my ego,
become hidden from myself, and arrive at placelessness.

❖ ❖ ❖ ❖

A cup is not enough — not even a pitcher!
Bring me a brimming cask without further delay![1]

Let me drink so much wine that I become Him,
that my entire being is filled up with Him.

Let me shed the bonds of acts and attributes,
and, once intoxicated, drink the pure wine of the Essence.[3]

Let me drink wine as never before,
that it may make me lose myself still more.

Let me drink so much wine that I become lost,
that the head of my being becomes joined to the cask.

Give such wine that I do not ask myself who I am
and become detached from future and past.

Let me go on, until in the valley of *faqr*
and *fana*, I lose all sense of my self.

Let me venture into the station of nothingness
and become freed from the bonds of self-importance.

❖ ❖ ❖ ❖

Give me that wine that burns up my self-existence
and effaces all I have.

Give me that wine that will not let me regain consciousness,
that keeps me from all thought of benefit and harm.

Give me that wine that plunders all that is,
leaving neither sobriety nor drunkenness!

Give me that wine that steals my voice,
that stops all my doubts and questions.

Give me that wine that sets me afire,
that I may remove the veil of the carnal self.

Give me that wine that burns all that I have
and spreads my ashes to the winds.

Give me that wine that hacks away at my roots
and dries up my desire and imagination.

Give me that wine that makes every particle Him,
that, when poured on a stone, makes it cry out "*Hu! Hu!*"

Give me that wine that makes me crazy,
that alienates me from all created beings.

❖ ❖ ❖ ❖

Give me that wine that puts multiplicity aside,
and through Divine Unity turns everything into Him.

Give me that wine that takes away my shadow-like existence,
so that the light of Divine Unity may nourish me in its embrace.

Give me that wine that sweeps away this wave,
that the Ocean of Unity may draw me into itself.

Give me that wine that plunders my form,
that dissolves completely all trace of my self-existence.

Let nothing be left of me but a dot,
so that people may know I'm no one at all.

Give me that wine that causes separation from self,
so that, distanced from self, my acts will be God's.

باران

Response Poems

RESPONSE TO A WAYFARER[1]

O friend, it is better to leave behind these imaginings and doubts;
    come with love and truly leave your self behind.
If you wish to escape the turbulence of the times
    and pass safely through the tavern of *fana* —
        it is necessary first to leave behind your self-identity.

I satisfied your thirst for a guide and by this delighted your heart.
    You escaped your cage and became free in my district.
Why then are you crying and wailing,
    trembling like a tree in the wind?
        It is better that you leave behind these sighs and groans.

I am unaware of myself, yet many are crazed with love for me.
    I am familiar with all, yet to all a stranger.
For how long will you moan for no reason about this fable of "I"?
    You who have become my moth, I am aware of your burning.
        The right course is to leave behind making a display of it.

Every wearied heart is my dwelling place of old.
    Within my chest, which is emptied of all resentment,
        lies the coffer of God's secret.
Benevolence to the helpless has for years been my occupation.
    My woolen cloak is the adornment of the eternal throne.
        You will see it plainly if you leave behind both worlds.

I am the remedy and the physician for your ailing heart.
    I am the captivator of the lovers' hearts and your beloved as well.
I am the cupbearer for the companions, and I am your commander,
    sometimes wrathful, sometimes benevolent — as I am your master.
        It is better that you leave behind your preference for "this" and "that."

Not until a heart bleeds will it be worthy of God.
    A heart will not become worthy of God until it is drenched in blood.
If the grapes are not transformed, wine cannot be made.
    What then can the heart become if it won't bleed?
        It is better for your heart to become bloodied so that you give up your life.

The drunkenness of the novice Magians[2] brings warmth to my marketplace.
    I make bleed the hearts of the *rendan* of this world.
Let him who desires me burn from separation or let him adapt,
    since either way he is my captive in this trap.
        Be patient, so that you will pass safely along this path.

For the greatest of lovers, union and separation are the same.
    For such patients, pain and cure are alike.
From the perspective of love, unbelief and faith clearly are one.
    Sometimes bubble, sometimes wave — Look, both are one!
        Leave behind doubt and you will find the way to certainty.

The discourse of the lovers is about the chain-like tress of my hair;
    their *zekr* is a wail caused by my enchanting face.
Their contemplation, day and night, is about my heart-soothing thought.
    Their eyes await a glance from the corner of my eyebrow.
        You must leave behind all imaginings and anxious thoughts.

Beware! I create turmoil for both stranger and friend.
    Beware! Without doubt, I know nothing of salve or sting.
From the former I am not soothed, from the latter not agitated.
    I am the bestower of light! Beware! This is my creed and practice.
        The condition is this: that you leave behind both loss and gain.

IN ANSWER TO A LETTER FROM A TRAVELER ON THE PATH

Seeking
O minstrel of the soul, for God's sake,
play the tuneless tune for a moment.

If the bond of loving-kindness is not present,
the heart will not hear our message.

How can the morning breeze by itself
bring a message to a friend?

May I always be love's companion;
perhaps then, I will explain fidelity

> and make drunk the sober companion
> that he might wake from fantasy and sleep.

Love
Whoever claims to have love for the Friend
should never feel sorry for himself.

Union and separation are the same to him,
so too infidelity and faith.

The lover has nothing but love, no thoughts
about having more or sadness from having less.

Until you gamble yourself away on love's path,
you will never be love's confidant.

> So, like Farhad[1], drunkenly wield the pick of *zekr*
> and cut through the mountain of self-existence!

Surrender
If you become surrendered to the Beloved,
don't think about union or separation.

Once you find your physician,
let neither pain nor cure concern you.

With all your heart and soul, be content and joyful
with whatever pleases the Beloved.

Go! Day and night, sit at the door of the heart!
Beware not to forget the image on the heart.[1]

> When your venture is ruined by this image,
> only then will your credit be increased.

Divine Unity
Here we are with the feast of love and drunkenness,
strangers to the bonds of self-worship.

In the banquet of devotion and loving-kindness,
the claim of self-existence is not heard.

From us, you will find no sign but the Beloved.
We are free from pride and shame.

No one is in our circle but God;
no stranger can break into our gathering.

> Satan did not leave his "I" and "we"[2] and so
> was rejected from the presence of the Beloved.

Union
The concept of self is but a passion;
God is not present in the house of "I" and "we."

God brought us to you, and you saw
that there is no claim other than the Truth.

Why do you seek God from other than God?
This is nothing but deception.

God can be sought from us, if you realize
that there is nothing but God.

> See us with eyes that do not suffer double vision,
> then seek God from us.

مرود

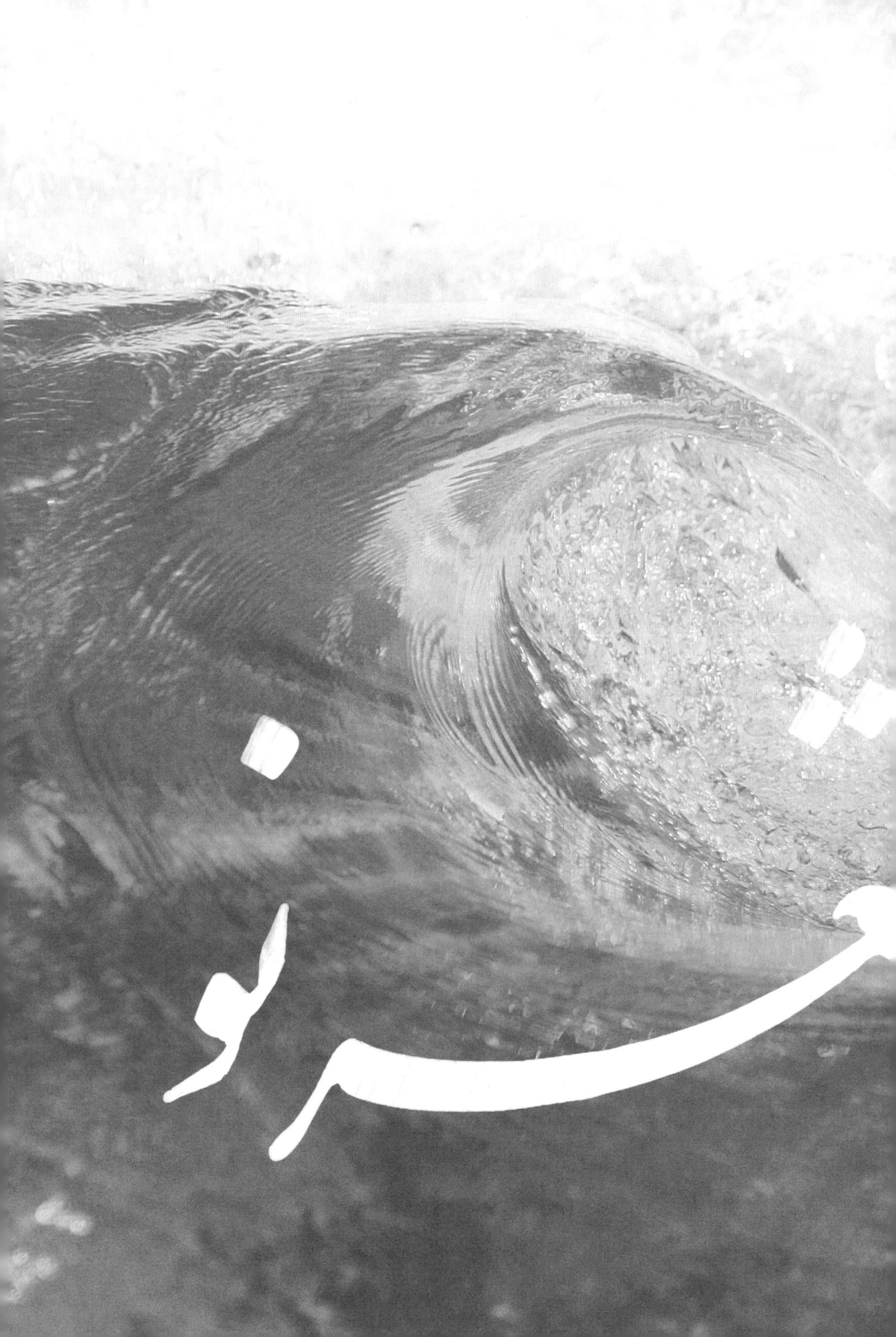

Persian New Verse

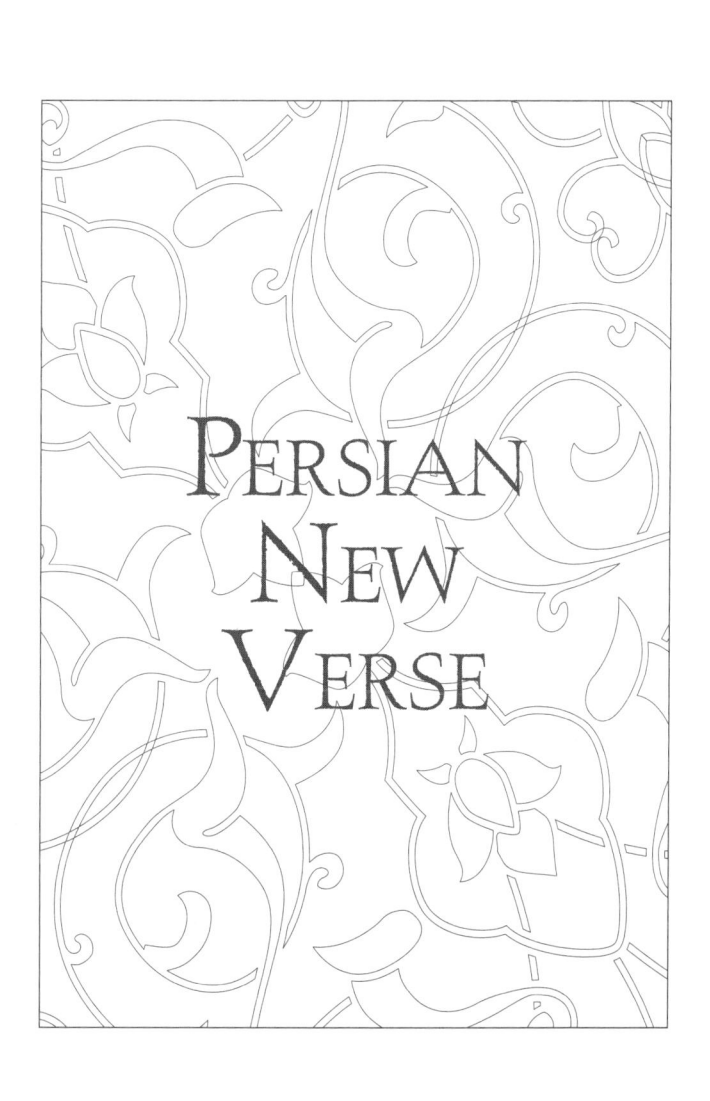

REMEMBERING YOU

Come...come... let's you and I
abandon the city of vultures,
        leave the region of "you" and "I"[1]
        and obtain a passport
        to the traceless realm,
Where no clocks are made
        and minutes are not sold,
Where the Khezr of good fortune
        has stitched pre- and post-eternity together,
Where they do not point to numbers
        and dust is not sold for gold,
Where breaths cannot be counted,
        where eternity, from end to end, is just one breath,
Where you
        will be I
        and I
        you.

YOU ARE MY POEM!

You!
With all your aloofness and pride
                You are my poem!
A poem...
                devoid of intellect.
                              Feeling!
                              Pure feeling
                              from the depth of being.

A poem that can never
                              be contained in words.

You asked of me free verse:
                You wanted...
A poem emerging from my heart
                without deliberation,
A fervor rising from my breast
                unembellished,
For all to see its nakedness
Devoid of everything that I am and have ever been,
                free of everything I know and have ever known,
                beyond the old and the new world.
So what is my free verse?
                Listen.........it is You!

BE SILENT!

A turbulent ocean,
        restless, in commotion,
        so much to tell, a chest-full, weighing me down
yet you say "Be silent!"
I talk
        not to think,
        not to pay attention to myself
        yet you say "Be silent!"
The atoms of my being
        are breaking apart
        I am exploding and becoming obliterated
        yet you say "Be silent!"
I pour my heart out
        only to amuse you;
        your joy makes me happy
                yet you say "Be silent!"
A starry-eyed child
        engages its mother with endless questions,
        the mother, oblivious to the child's need and joy, responds
                "Hush, be silent!"

OCEAN

Infinite Ocean.
        All water!
                All water!

You are finite…
        so you envision Him to be finite too.

Intricate patterns,
        not yours

Rather, planets, solar systems and galaxies.
        You are an invisible speck.
        Who are you? You are nothing!

And everything you have
        And your earth;
        nothing upon nothing!

He has been in motion from pre-eternity
        to post-eternity without end;
        one wave subsides
                another surges.

Demolish the form,
        break the mold,

The form of imagination,
        the mold of the dream of existence.

Hear from the Ocean
        the true song of creation:

There was the Ocean
        and nothing else;

And there is only the Ocean
        and nothing else.

باعبّات

QUATRAINS

THE QUATRAINS

Unless they know You through Your eyes
    they cannot know You in all that is manifest.
Those who think they know You by their thoughts
    are either far from You or do not know You at all.

❖ ❖ ❖ ❖

I have given both worlds to buy You;
    I have fled myself and chosen You.
I have closed my heart to all except You;
    whatever I look at, I see only You.

❖ ❖ ❖ ❖

Heaven for me is to behold Your face —
    when I'm away from You everything is ugly to me.
I am in the sleep of life and dream of You —
    I have no concern about the Kaaba or cloister.

❖ ❖ ❖ ❖

My heart desires to behold the Beloved;
    my face has two weeping eyes.
My mind yearns for union with Him;
    my body holds a restless soul.

❖ ❖ ❖ ❖

It is clear that life means nothing without You;
    without the vision of Your face, eternal life means nothing.
Your love gives me new life every moment;
    without Your love these transitory days mean nothing.

❖ ❖ ❖ ❖

This imaginary existence, this "I" and "you,"[1] is nothing but a sip
    from the ocean of which "you" and "I" is but one cup.
The accomplished on this path have left no trace —
    only the imperfect leave traces of "you" and "I."

❖ ❖ ❖ ❖

In the circle of existence Being is but one;
    all existence is but an image on water — Being is but one.
If you dissolve in the ocean of *fana*,
    you'll see that ocean, bubble, drop and river are one.

❖ ❖ ❖ ❖

In the eyes of a *qalandar*, the world is just a dream
    and to expect prosperity from the world is absurd.
To think, even momentarily, about oneself is idolatry,
    as the self-important are considered idol-worshipers.

❖ ❖ ❖ ❖

So long as you care about being accepted or rejected by others
    I don't believe that you have any faith in remembrance of God.
You will not find what is hidden unless
    you become absent to all that is around you.

❖ ❖ ❖ ❖

We have no thought of good or bad;
    whether someone is a friend or foe makes no difference to us.
We are a mirror for all those who look upon us —
    they see in us whatever is in themselves.

❖ ❖ ❖ ❖

In the book of love, there is no mention of "I" and "we."[2]
    He who dies to "I" and "we" lives in love.
With all your self-importance, do not talk of love.
    Silence! You have not understood who the lover is.

❖ ❖ ❖ ❖

The people of this world have bodies that lack heart;
    to them, talk of love and devotion is not pleasing.
O people of vision, find a solution —
    humanity hardly exists, and no one can do much about it.

❖ ❖ ❖ ❖

The heart that has never been in love is not a heart;
    if it does not love, then it is just a lump of clay.[3]
Love is the truth and all else is false;
    thus, for the lover of truth the false does not exist.

❖ ❖ ❖ ❖

One who is alive through love can never die;
    he is not a prisoner of these few days of life.
He whose heart tastes the salve of love
    has a soul that will not succumb to the sting of death.

❖ ❖ ❖ ❖

O cupbearer, bring me the wine that takes away self-existence
    and all thoughts of self-worship,
the wine that either blinds my eyes to fantasies
    or opens my eyes and takes away my drunkenness.

❖ ❖ ❖ ❖

You have said that you will torment people
    and make them fear the day of judgment.
I am certain that no anguish can come from You —
    that is why we don't believe that You will punish anyone.

❖ ❖ ❖ ❖

O cupbearer, bring me the wine that burns away my being,
    the wine that will take away my hopes for elevation
        and my fears of humiliation,
the wine that makes me forget my drunkenness,
    the wine that consumes itself and its worshiper.

❖ ❖ ❖ ❖

In union there is always fear of separation;
    in separation there is always hope for union.
It is best for me to leave both fear and hope
    and want only what the Beloved wants.

❖ ❖ ❖ ❖

One cannot depend on the love of anybody;
    one cannot give one's heart to just any lowlife.
Beware! Do not fall in love with any good-for-nothing
    or become bewitched by the charm of an inwardly bankrupt imposter.

❖ ❖ ❖ ❖

As long as you seek to be recognized as good,
    or to be known as capable, pure and well-mannered,
do not speak of the Ocean before the *qalandaran*!
    Though they let you sit with them, they know you are no more than a stream.

❖ ❖ ❖ ❖

There is one Being with manifold manifestations —
    there will never be any other apart from that One.
His creation is a manifestation of Him;
    God exists; created beings do not.

❖ ❖ ❖ ❖

One cannot treat the people of purity with anything other than purity;
    one cannot deal with the selfless through one's ego.
Although *qalandaran* are unaware of their selves,
    one cannot become their companion through pretense.

❖ ❖ ❖ ❖

Your knowledge is but a veil for you;
    the fruit of fantasy is nothing but a dream.
If you see there is no ocean, no wave and no bubble,
    then you will see only water when you look.

❖ ❖ ❖ ❖

Once again I gave up hope in all that exists,
    and in neediness I have directed my gaze towards Your benevolence.
O You who are kin for those who have no one,
    I shall not reach out to anyone but You.

❖ ❖ ❖ ❖

I ride this earth like a steed, night and day;
    I am steadfast on the path to union with You, night and day.
In order to reach You I drive ego away from myself;
    I am fleeing from the district of "I" and "you"[4] night and day.

❖ ❖ ❖ ❖

Stay alone, and escape from others without hesitation.
    Be selfless and flee all "I" and "we."[5]
Whenever you stumble upon blind-hearted people
    either become deaf and dumb or run away.

❖ ❖ ❖ ❖

Whosoever knows You has nothing to do with others.
    The grace of Your transforming glance drives him away from them.
When Your essence is witnessed by one who knows You,
    he comes to know the rest as utter non-being.

❖ ❖ ❖ ❖

The one who came to know You became free from himself;
    the one who became detached from himself attached himself to You.
When the ocean-hearted Sufi saw Your ocean,
    out of purity and sincerity he washed his hands of himself.

❖ ❖ ❖ ❖

Through love I was liberated from my own being and non-being;
    in desiring You, I fastened my heart to love.
Ultimately, I had no other aim. Away from everyone,
    I am sitting down again with love.

❖ ❖ ❖ ❖

I offered up my heart and soul on the path of love;
    I offered up my attachment to wife and children, house and home.
To be admitted in the tavern of annihilation
    I gave up thinking about any of these things.

❖ ❖ ❖ ❖

I have seen the conditions of this world and all its attractions and rejections,
    from its wealth and poverty to its warmth and cold.
I realized it was all but a dream, whether good or bad.
    To me, whoever lets go of the world is valiant.

❖ ❖ ❖ ❖

Like grapes, we have always accompanied the vat.
    We have disappeared from the eyes of the world.
For years we boiled from the fire of love
    until we became that wine that intoxicates all.

❖ ❖ ❖ ❖

What a place I have found in a corner of the tavern of ruin!
    I continually drink with them who have no news of themselves.
Since we have left behind the path of spiritual stations and miraculous powers,
    we celebrate and are forever joyful.

❖ ❖ ❖ ❖

In the ocean of being, we are restless waves;
    the sea is in motion and we are bewildered.
Though in appearance we are wave, bubble and foam,
    in reality we are all water, and this we know.

❖ ❖ ❖ ❖

I gave my heart to You, so that my soul could find rest,
    then I gave You my soul, so my heart would not be anxious.
"How strange!" the calculating intellect said to itself,
    "In the business of love the profit is in loss."

❖ ❖ ❖ ❖

Love is the foundation for the existence of everything.
> Without love there would be no trace of either world.

Through love, you are the light and the bestower of light.
> Be aware that without love you are neither.

❖ ❖ ❖ ❖

I love You through remembrance when far from You.
> I offered up my heart and soul to soften Your pride.

I am telling You what You already know:
> that for me being separated and far away from You is hard.

❖ ❖ ❖ ❖

The eye that sees You sees everything.
> The heart that is attentive to You ignores the rest.

He who does not know You knows no one.
> He who knows You knows everyone.

❖ ❖ ❖ ❖

We are images on water, for water is all we are.
> Only the One is awake, while we are all asleep.

O cupbearer, bring us cup after cup!
> Only the One is sober, while we are all dead drunk!

❖ ❖ ❖ ❖

We are all under the control of God's will;
> we are all clenched in the grip of His wrath.

We asked, "Who are we?" He smiled and said,
> "Stop this nonsense; we are all one."[6]

❖ ❖ ❖ ❖

Without love, you are dead, even if alive.
> Without love, you are base, even if cherished.

Without love, you are wretched, even if you are a king.
> With love, you are a commander, even if you appear to be helpless.

❖ ❖ ❖ ❖

Unless you gamble all on the path of love,
> refrain from trespassing on the banquet of purity;

Unless you abandon the illusory "I" and "we"[7]
> You are not allowed into the tavern of ruin.

❖ ❖ ❖ ❖

When I sleep, You are the center of my dreams;
    when I wake up You are the reason for my fervor.
O You the possessor of my sleeping and waking,
    You are both my bewitching trap and my captivator.

❖ ❖ ❖ ❖

You will not seek pain unless you are valiant.
    You will not seek a master unless you have pain.
Beware, don't be fooled into
    following a false master.

❖ ❖ ❖ ❖

In the realm of love, do not search for anything but the Beloved.
    As long as you are aware of yourself, do not talk of the Beloved.
Travel the path where craziness and drunkenness are the guides.
    Beware! Do not keep company with those who are sober.

❖ ❖ ❖ ❖

المحبّة في وثائق الوُحدة

Truths of Love

TRUTHS OF LOVE 1

This is our religion: to perpetually call out
to God within the heart,

to efface ourselves from thought,
but never forget His Name,

hearts never heedless of the Friend,
fidelity always impressed in memory.

It is spiritual savor that nurtures devotion;
it is pain that bestows purity.

O pain, stay! God is the physician.
Seek not a cure! God is generous.

TRUTHS OF LOVE 2

O Sublime, Ever-Living, Self-Subsistent, Unique One,
transcending all descriptions!

You ravage the hearts of lovers
and plunder the life of the soul.

Your Indian beauty mark[1] appears in every age,
consuming our souls like aloes wood in its censer.

The cries of the wayfarers slain in Your district
resound perpetually as far as the highest heaven.

Every instant You appear dressed in a different guise,
driving us mad and ravishing our hearts.

TRUTHS OF LOVE 3

Are You so unaware of the heart's distress
that you twist Your braid so coquettishly?

Your dark eyes have ambushed my faith.
I feel like a stranger now wherever I go.

I have fallen behind in traveling the path, caught in a maelstrom
churning within the sea of bewilderment.

Either seize what life is left to me
or rescue me, the drowned one in Your ocean!

You captivate my heart and then bid me wait,
to languish in love without impatience.

TRUTHS OF LOVE 4

O chief mullah of the city, stop insinuating
that our school brings ruin.

Many seek us by means of the intellect
but cannot find our path.

Your religion is self-worship;
our path is selflessness.

Close your lips to empty chatter;
this matter lies beyond your comprehension.

The bird of our heart flies with the wind,
yearning to reach the Divine Hunter.

TRUTHS OF LOVE 5

I said, "To see Your beauty
I will polish the rust from my heart's mirror

so Your reflection may be cast within it
and I will be ready to converse with You."

What immature thoughts these were!
What mirror? What seeking?

Alas, this way of thinking itself was my veil!
My desire for You is absurd.

No longer will I crave to see You,
for in *fana* alone lies the answer.

TRUTHS OF LOVE 6

That brazen, drunken Beloved has stolen my religion
through the unbelief inspired by Her curls.

When She sees a careless aspirant
She breaks his legs and withholds a helping hand!

Ah, the countless lovers' hearts pierced
by the darts flung from Her eyelashes!

We have surrendered ourselves to Her unconditionally,
forsaking our hearts, offering up our souls.

Perhaps now She will drive us away from egotism
and set us free from self-existence.

TRUTHS OF LOVE 7

I will sit by the heart's threshold, O Friend,
sanctifying its ruins with Your name.

I will trace the image of Your visage upon my heart
until I clearly see You rising[2] there.

I will call out "*Haqq, Haqq!*" repeatedly
until Your message is proclaimed from my heart's Kaaba.

In the heart's shade, intimate with You,
I will drink down with purity Your ever-flowing wine.

All this will I do until I turn the house of my heart into rubble
and gamble away all my being on Your path.

TRUTHS OF LOVE 8

It has been a long time since, through the tribulations of Your love,
we were freed from the trials of the world.

You are the one we yearn for, and
You are the one who created this longing.

We have passed from self for You,
since there was no one else who mattered.

Stop asking us about vices, mullah!
We don't talk about anything but Him.

Ah, what is the use of discussion and debate?
Leave us to delight in our ecstatic states.

TRUTHS OF LOVE 9

O heart, how conceited you are about your knowledge!
Beware! Love is the true way.

Only when you give up "I" and "we"[3] in tribute
will the Beloved lay down His head in reconciliation.

Your knowledge will be completely transformed into vision
when your self-existence is plundered.

Never will you see the Beloved
until you expel all but Him from the heart.

No one can enter the Beloved's abode,
just as a piece of wood cannot reach the depths of the sea.

TRUTHS OF LOVE 10

There is a difference between those who circle the heart within
and those who perform the outward motions of the hajj.

Annihilation of the self is the way of the former;
the latter endeavor to correct pronunciation.

Why persist in arguing with such false pretenders?
Unaware of the mysteries, they will always remain obstinate.

They profess to follow the "straight path,"
so why do they proceed so crookedly?

As long as their eyes see double
they will lack true vision.

TRUTHS OF LOVE 11

On both the way of religion and the mystical path
the Truth is always the ultimate aim.

To my eyes that see only Unity,
nothing but the Friend is manifest.

Ask not about news of "others"
from the person who has no news of himself.

No trace at all remains of that one
who has drowned in the sea of *fana*.

God alone abides eternally —
this much should suffice if you possess a heart.

TRUTHS OF LOVE 12

How can someone who has not reformed himself
ever think about improving others?

People see their beloved's image in me,
since I am a light for all.

Your profit is in proportion to your capacity,
so stop your pointless insistence!

Your goal is not outside yourself;
in your own locked being lies the key.

With purity, journey inward, away from self,
and gaze upon the Kaaba of His face.

TRUTHS OF LOVE 13

From the start I closed my own account
so that the Beloved's matters took precedence.

With purity, I defeated myself
so that my heart's struggle ended in victory.

When I turned against myself,
blame for me became praise.

With eyes that see Unity I looked and saw Him as the point
from which all possible dimensions originate.

Here there is no place left for talk;
it is evident that no one but Him exists.

TRUTHS OF LOVE 14

Seek within yourself the rose that you desire!
How long will you hop from branch to bough like a nightingale?

Yield and be pliant in the grip of love,
for the brazen aspirant will be crushed!

Ah, never have you endured the sting of love's cruelty
nor savored its kindness.

Palaces and shacks are equal
in the eyes of one who yearns for the Beloved:

Wherever he goes, there is love.
Wherever he looks, he sees love's sign.

TRUTHS OF LOVE 15

He who seeks the world for its own sake
will forever be preoccupied with its fantasies.

The ascetic will not surrender to this world;
restlessly, he hurries to the hereafter.

Sometimes he takes pride in his prayers;
sometimes he takes pleasure in thoughts of paradise with its virgins.

But we have fled from both worlds,
awaiting whatever melody the Beloved will play.

Though we are captivated by the curl of the Beloved,
through love's passion, we are sovereign.

TRUTHS OF LOVE 16

Ascetics seek virgins in heaven through prayers;
in humble entreaty, we seek Him alone.

Let those who deny us know
we have already rejected ourselves.

I adore this gamble of love,
for the penniless profit from their loss.

Whoever plays His backgammon of love
never rests until he gambles himself away.

So long as the dice are rolled by the Cupbearer,
the lovers will lie stranded in an impasse[4] of bewilderment.

TRUTHS OF LOVE 17

Since the pen of love was set in motion,
I have been putting words to paper.

As the nights of separation darkened,
so the white pages filled with writing.

Yet even after a hundred thousand pages,
the book of love did not reach its end.

I saw that when compared with the lover's worth
those pages had no value.

Love made the pen falter and in jealousy
washed away all that had been written.

TRUTHS OF LOVE 18

That mischievous, trouble-stirring Beloved
displays a different face every moment.

He is the plunderer of the clever, sober ones,
ravaging religion and hearts with each breath in a different way.

He prescribes a different cure
for the patient on each occasion.

Every instant, He opens another shop
for the sake of each customer.

He deals in wares of every kind,
all so that our self-existence may be driven from us.

TRUTHS OF LOVE 19

I said this to myself: "Once union is attained
I shall not leave the Beloved for one moment!"

Do not be surprised if, on the way of fidelity, you meet
with torment before the Beloved can be embraced.

Water that flows down to the ocean
must twist and turn and rise and fall.

This lovely secret that was always in view
I committed to memory with so much joy.

When the Beloved set foot in my district,
my wish vanished like an image on water.

TRUTHS OF LOVE 20

We have talked a lot about love, but we have
still not taken even the first step in describing love.

O love! You transcend all description:
this, in brief, is the only way to describe you.

No one other than you knows anything about you;
we can never unravel this mystery.

Through you, God manifests His divinity!
Who can claim a miracle surpassing this?

Silence! Shrouding love's name
excels by far any word of praise.

TRUTHS OF LOVE 21

Love! Come! I will sacrifice my soul to You!
Reason, get up and leave!

O cupbearer at the banquet of lovers,
come, pour me a cup overflowing with wine

so I may shatter this talisman *"La"*[5]
and refrain forever from further repentance.

That one who is unaware of self
is also unaware of everything other than God.

Whatever choices he makes come from love;
love, too, is the source of all his ways.

TRUTHS OF LOVE 22

All that we have comes from the inspiration
received from the breath of the perfected ones.

Through the grace of the Beloved, we have emerged
from myriad forms into the realm of the attributes.

When we bound our hearts to the love of His face,
we broke free from everything.

The drunken lovers see no difference
between satin and sackcloth.

The one who is enamored with the Beloved
is a stranger to both husk and kernel.

TRUTHS OF LOVE 23

The ocean of the mystic's being
can never be polluted by a mere chip of wood.

The pure robes of the friends of God
can never be stained by someone with a dark heart.

This allusion should suffice
if anyone is home in the house of your heart.

You have passed a lifetime in forgetfulness;
if you now feel pain, then enough of this negligence.

Join our assembly, valiantly
flee from yourself to be with God!

TRUTHS OF LOVE 24

The Sufi exists for the Beloved;
the world exists for the Sufi.

Although the god of most people is but an idol,
I saw that the Sufi's lord is truly God.

If you wish to truly prostrate before God,
bow in the dust at the Sufi's feet.

Since the Sufi's place is everywhere,
God declared, "Wherever you turn is My face."[6]

If the Sufi himself is not God,
he is certainly not separate from God.

TRUTHS OF LOVE 25

We yearn for You, and for Your torment too.
For us, the stings felt on Your path are but salve.

Whoever is afflicted by Your love
is never disturbed by reason.

One who is overcome by Your love
shatters the talisman of religion and creed.

No real lover ever sought out heart or religion
after he found Your love within himself.

Since love is the true religion and way,
God continually bestows His splendor upon it.

TRUTHS OF LOVE 26

In the dominion of love and devotion,
our wealth lies in being sincere.

Only sincerity succeeds in love;
by sincerity the ordinary are turned into the elect.

When we put on sincerity's garb,
we became divers in the ocean of love.

In the ledger of love, sincerity alone
provides the balance for one's credit.

Don't approach love and drunkenness without sincerity
lest your actions lead you to degradation.

TRUTHS OF LOVE 27

Whatever your disguise, the man of God
will always recognize you.

If it's a self-gratifying remedy you're after, go away!
The grace of the Merciful is not for everyone.

O wayfarer, as long as you see imperfection,
you'll be pointing to your own flaws.

Be without self; be with Him —
this, in brief, is our aim.

Forget remedies; pursue pain!
Abandon your own goal; seek a man of God!

TRUTHS OF LOVE 28

For me, everything but God is worthless.
How fruitless then is this debate over fatalism and free will.

I urge my love-stricken disciples on
toward the district of the Beloved.

If someone lacks sincerity what good
would it do for me to change their *zekr*?

In love's banquet, beggar and king are equal,
for there is no discrimination here.

To the one who speaks from sincerity,
I reveal the hidden mysteries of love.

TRUTHS OF LOVE 29

Go! Try to find the source of contraction[7] within yourself!
It is not an excuse to say that God brings on this state.

Do not forget the primordial covenant.[8]
Do not break this promise with your unfaithfulness.

You look up to yourself without realizing
you have no greater foe than yourself.

There is no problem in the world but you;
it is your self-existence that obscures your view.

Do not see your self, and then you will see,
through His eyes, all things as they truly are.[9]

TRUTHS OF LOVE 30

The lover is not separate from the Beloved;
there is no arbiter between them.

Wash away the contraction inflicted by self
with Unity's water, and seize the ready cash of expansion.[10]

Pass beyond yourself, then realize that you are He.
Do not worry about a balanced approach.

In ascending to the summit of human potential,
there is a danger of falling from nearness.

So until you have reached the final destination,
you must not rest even for a moment.

TRUTHS OF LOVE 31

Why do people advise me about love?
This is a matter for the heart only.

"A lover sets no conditions," they say,
but they do not live up to that obligation.

The heart is a goblet in which the world is revealed;
the heart is not made of flesh and blood.

Though men describe the heart in great detail,
they have yet to explain even one of its attributes.

Only the possessor of a heart with full awareness,
can ever exclaim, "I have a time with God."[11]

TRUTHS OF LOVE 32

With the eyes of selfhood, you cannot see Him,
for His face is reserved for Himself alone.

Not until you annihilate "I" and "we"[12]
will you have any luck with Him.

The lover says all without speaking,
for love is beyond all that can be said.

Not every ignorant fool can be a selfless mystic;
this is a principle to be borne in mind.

Beware, do not seize the hem of some worthless person's cloak;
avoid being ruined by someone slain by his own ego.

TRUTHS OF LOVE 33

The soul listened to the exclamation, "Yes!"[13]
not to the rival's rebuke or the preacher's counsel.

That is why, day and night, it stands watchful,
like Mahmud, over the secret of the Ayaz of the heart.[14]

My heart was lost when its Beloved gazed
with the eye of "He is the All-Seeing."[15]

I have gone, and like Hafez
there remains of us only a tale of love,

until the turn of someone else comes,
bringing with it the story of another love.

TRUTHS OF LOVE 34

I have separated from the people of the intellect
to join the companions of love.

When love's legend reached my ears
I recited a requiem for myself.

When love's banner was raised up
intellect's standard was cast down.

Truth arrived and falsehood departed.[16]
Love arrived and the intellect was overthrown.

Love came to reign over the heart's realm
and intellect, feeling ashamed, gave up its boastful claim.

TRUTHS OF LOVE 35

We are beyond whatever
people say about us.

Do not ask us which religious school we follow;
be content with your own.

In love's school there is only the One;
the speaker is no other than the listener.

The shadow we once cast is now traceless,
vanished in the sunlight of His face.

Shadow? What shadow? It was but a fantasy
that in ignorance imagined itself to be real.

TRUTHS OF LOVE 36

Not until your heart becomes empty of everything else
will you be able to turn towards God.

How many elders are but infants in love!
How many youths have been made adepts by love!

Only the Beloved can paint you
with the hue of a lover.

Many people have spent fortunes
attempting in vain to replicate that color.

Lifetimes they wasted wavering with doubts,
and in the end we saw that they had just painted themselves.

TRUTHS OF LOVE 37

When I escaped from self by remembrance of You,
I became free from all chatter and debate.

O mullah, if clever speech is your attainment,
then I am free from such an accomplishment.

I look upon the faces of the beautiful
but have no concern for make-up, beauty mark or curl.[17]

Most people pursue fantasies.
I am free from all such illusion.

Filled with madness, drunkenness and love,
I am a stranger to the bonds of self-worship.

TRUTHS OF LOVE 38

Where Sufis are assembled,
Gabriel himself descends to serve.

The profane consider it forbidden
to listen to the sound of tambourine and lute,

yet during the *sama* of the lovers of Divine Unity,
even the angels in the empyrean clap along.

At the sound of *sama*, love's winged steed[18]
soars beyond all dimensions.

The one who has no desires remaining
has nothing to experience but joy.

TRUTHS OF LOVE 39

Until you come to know yourself,
you will never know the Beloved.

There are many who circle the Kaaba,
but try to find one who circles the heart instead.

How will you wake to the Beloved
when you remain unaware of the heart?

Go! For God's sake, discover the Beloved!
Esoteric symbols will not reveal Him.

Notice the dot placed among the letters;[19]
now rest securely like that dot.

TRUTHS OF LOVE 40

Because the Beloved yearned for us,
we likewise fell in love with Him.

Since the Day of the Covenant and that fateful "Yes!"[20]
we have honored our pledge.

This is our custom:
we accept everyone's religion.

Alas, there is not a single physician in the city
with the skill to cure our pain.

For God's sake, O pretenders,
question us no more about our state!

TRUTHS OF LOVE 41

No will of my own exists any longer.
I am content with whatever pleases the Beloved.

I have closed my accounts with everyone
so I can devote myself fully to the Beloved.

Once I became a stranger to all of creation
I saw that whatever exists is God.

Were they to taste my overpowering wine
people would repent from their own repentance!

Those who became free from the vanity of fragrance and color
drank down the wine and smashed the pitcher.

TRUTHS OF LOVE 42

Alas, the lovers of this day and age
are skeptical of their own love!

Today only a legend remains of love,
yet this fable will never be abandoned.

Though the lovers' ardor is now diminished,
this burning passion will never be extinguished.

Love, which had always reigned as king,
has become a slave in our era.

We have seen that in every age it was enslaved,
love itself planted the sapling of loving.

TRUTHS OF LOVE 43

That one who is unconscious of self
can never fear another.

Annihilated from self, I have been freed
from all losses and gains in this world of dust.

The one who is drowned in love's ocean
sees only the water of Divine Unity.

In the eyes of the lover, a wrecked heart is worth
more than a thousand gardens and orchards.

I have God in my heart,
and I am joyful in my heart's delight.

TRUTHS OF LOVE 44

How long will you follow this one and that?
Your aim will never be attained through others.

Step forward with devotion and enter
the inner sanctuary of the heart's Kaaba!

Seek within yourself what you want
and thereby resolve your numerous problems.

A hundred precious treasures lie hidden within you,
yet this temporal playground has obstructed your vision.

Observe the ocean contained inside a pitcher
and look in the mirror of His essence and attributes.[21]

TRUTHS OF LOVE 45

Better to say nothing at all of love, O heart,
than to say something useless.

What do you know of the bond of love, O heart,
except vain fantasy and idle dreams?

If the mirror becomes polished, O heart,
there will be no more distinction between lover and Beloved.

When the Beloved manifests Himself, O heart,
the lover will be annihilated.

A wave surged up in the ocean, crying, "No power exists
but through God,"[22] then merged with the ocean once again.

TRUTHS OF LOVE 46

When I become drunk on His wine,
I find freedom from the thought of gain and loss.

Unceasingly I drink the dregs of pain for Him.
My only sorrow is grief caused by Him.

I regard as a godsend
each breath that I remember the Beloved.

Through the Beloved's attraction and my longing to see Him,
I surrender both worlds to love.

I see that where a trace of "we" and "you"[23] remains
it is to the detriment of love.

TRUTHS OF LOVE 47

If you want to see God
take a step outside yourself.

You shall attain to God's greatest name
once you forget your own name.

If your cup is indeed never empty of wine,
where is your warmth, drunkenness and madness?

Go, set no more traps on people's paths.
You will not profit from bait and snare.

Become prey, not stalker!
Watch out for the fetters and chains!

TRUTHS OF LOVE 48

I shall speak no more of separation
since such is the Beloved's preference.

Union that is achieved by my own desire
will never resolve my heart's predicament.

I shall not submit to anyone else again,
even if love's flames consume my very soul.

I am lovesick, and my Beloved is the physician,
whether in union or separation, with pain or with cure.

Do not express your opinion about the game of love,
for in truth love is not a game.

TRUTHS OF LOVE 49

To those who look with the eyes of the intellect,
we followers of love appear mad.

When love's centerpoint began to revolve,
the intellect quit the circle.

We saw that the intellect was stunned
before the one bewitched by love.

That *rend* who wagers all he owns
is never defeated in love's game.

He has a place set in love's presence,
having gambled himself away and won God.

TRUTHS OF LOVE 50

Do not consider yourself so important, O Kaaba,
for I see the Beloved in every district.

With my lips placed firmly upon the Beloved's,
braid and curl no longer entice me.

Resting in the embrace of the source of all motion
I no longer feel a need to search and explore.

Nor does concern for discussion remain:
the Beloved speaks to me about myself.

When I shook off the dust of selfhood
I saw that nothing remained of me but Him.

TRUTHS OF LOVE 51

Rise! Step into our circle;
sit as a companion at our banquet.

Take goblet in hand with remembrance of His face;
free yourself from the thought of anything else.

Stop twisting around yourself like an unripe bud —
drink down this wine and blossom into a flower.

Then, let go of the hem of selfhood's garment
and become acquainted with the early morning breeze

Until you find yourself far from both color and fragrance
and become joyful in your own annihilation.

TRUTHS OF LOVE 52

Everything I see is imbued
with Your beautiful face.

You are there, whether hidden or revealed;
the rest is but fable and dream.

You are the one being worshiped, whether in mosque,
church or temple: all these places are but pretexts.

The people of the heart found nothing
but the treasure of You in their hearts, O Unique Pearl.

There is sugar only on Your ruby lips —
all the rest is just a crooked smile.

TRUTHS OF LOVE 53

I have shut tight the book of "heart and Beloved,"
transcended all talk of "wayfarers and paths."

He who has no awareness of himself
is also unaware of "we" and "you."[24]

He who is unaware of day or night
is a stranger to both sun and moon.

Because we were love's slaves,
we have become monarchs in the realm of loving.

No matter that we lack an army,
we are commanding kings in the dominion of the heart.

TRUTHS OF LOVE 54

Smash the goblet! Let go of the pitcher!
How long will you remain self-indulgently drunk at love's banquet?

If you drink wine but never gamble yourself away,
how will you ever cast your self-existence to the wind?

O you brazen one! Reaching out with a rude hand
is not permitted at the table of purity.

If you have indeed abandoned idolatry,
why then do you hold on to all these idols?

You have transgressed as well,
exempting yourself from loyalty!

TRUTHS OF LOVE 55

Look not for a trace of me in the world:
my only trace is tracelessness.

I was a captive in the realm of His love
for a while in a time of timelessness.

For years I drank wine with the Beloved
alone in a place of placelessness.

Since the end of all speech is silence,
listen to the speech of speechlessness.

Rise! Step out of the way,
so the Beloved may enter your house.

NOTES

Page 3:   1. See "we" and "you" in the Glossary.
Page 8:   2. Arabic: *ana 'l-Haqq* ("I am the Truth"), the ecstatic saying of Hallaj, regarding whom see the Glossary.
Page 10:   1. See "I" and "you" in the Glossary.
Page 13:   1. "The master of the Magi" refers to the master of the spiritual path. See J. Nurbakhsh, *Sufi Symbolism*, Vol. III, p.218.
Page 19:   1. The divine fiat, the way in which God is repeatedly described in the Qur'an as granting created things existence, before which they are described as non-existents in a storehouse. See, e.g., Qur'an 16:40, 15:21. The original is a Persian translation of Qur'an 17:81.
Page 20:   2. Literally, Mahmud, concerning whom see "Mahmud and Ayaz" in the Glossary.
Page 24:   1. *mashhad*, which means both a place of martyrdom and a place where people gather to witness; it is also the name of a city in northeastern Iran where the shrine of Imam Reza, the 8th Shi'ite imam, is located.
           2. The name *Reza* literally means "contentment."
Page 26:   1. A Persian version of Qur'an 2:115: "Wherever you turn there is the face of God."
           2. Arabic: *ana 'l-Haqq* ("I am the Truth"), the ecstatic saying of Hallaj, regarding whom see the Glossary.
Page 27:   1. *mahv*, which means effacement of the being of the individual.
           2. *tams*, which means extinction of the traces of attributes and essence.
           3. *sahv*, which means return of the power of discrimination.
Page 33:   1. See "I" and "you" in the Glossary.
Page 34:   1. Literally, the Homa bird, the shadow of the Homa bird being a frequently used motif in Persian literature. The Homa is a mythical bird comparable to the phoenix, but particularly associated with soaring at the highest levels of the heavens and bestowing kingship on those who are under its shadow.
Page 37:   1. See "I" and "we" in the Glossary.
           2. Arabic: *ana 'l-Haqq* ("I am the Truth"), the ecstatic saying of Hallaj, regarding whom see the Glossary.
Page 41:   1. The Persian word *mansur*, translated here as "victorious," is also the name of the Sufi Mansur Hallaj who was famously hung from the gallows. See further "Hallaj" in the Glossary.
Page 42:   1. Zoroastrian priest.
Page 43:   1. Arabic: *ana 'l-Haqq* ("I am the Truth"), the ecstatic saying of Hallaj, regarding whom see the Glossary
Page 45:   1. See "I" and "you" in the Glossary.
Page 46:   1. This verse alludes to the biblical and Qur'anic story about Moses and the burning bush and also more specifically to the following verse by Hafez: "I am not the only one who is made cheerful by the fire in Sinai;/Moses comes here hoping for an ember." In Sufi literature Moses represents knowledge of exoteric religion, which cannot comprehend or cope with mystical knowledge and experience (e.g. Moses and Khezr in the Qur'an; Moses and the Shepherd in Rumi's *Masnavi*).
Page 48:   1. See "I" and "we" in the Glossary.
Page 50:   1. See "we" and "I" in the Glossary.
Page 51:   1. The tower and gate signify the entrance to the seat of authority and power to the realm. Here, the watchtower and the gate are built from the heads and hearts of the exalted ones (lovers) who have ventured here. Hence, the price of entry is the wayfarer's individual self-existence.
Page 54:   1. This line could also mean, "I swear by Your Friendship."
           2. See "I" and "we" in the Glossary.

NOTES

Page 55   1. *safa*, which also means "integrity."
            2. *sokhra*, which also means "exploited" or "taken into forced labor."
            3. See "I" and "you" in the Glossary.
Page 56:   1. See "I" and "you" in the Glossary.
Page 57:   1. See "I" and "we" in the Glossary.
Page 58:   1. *sarjoosh*, which literally means "head boil" but when used in context means (i) the froth or cream that rises to the top when some liquids boil, (ii) the basic, the choice, the optimal or (iii) a choice and excellent wine.
Page 60:   1. An expounder of religious law.
Page 62:   1. The letter *alef* in the Persian alphabet is a vertical line.
            2. The letter *dal* in the Persian alphabet looks similar to an English *c*, so it resembles a vertical line that has bent over from half-way down.
            3. The letter *nun* in the Persian alphabet takes the form of *u* in English and is written below most other letters.
            4. This is a reference to the cane used by members of the exoteric clergy in the past to punish those they accused of heresy.
Page 63:   1. The Qur'an is traditionally divided into 30 equal parts for the benefit of reciters.
            2. See "Layli and Majnun" in the Glossary.
            3. Here the title "sheikh" refers to an exoteric religious leader.
            4. The terms used here to describe the soul becoming a tyrant are *nafs* and *ammara*, alluding specifically to the tyrannical soul that commands one to gratify its desires. See J. Nurbakhsh, *The Psychology of Sufism* and also his *Sufi Symbolism*, Vol. IX, p. 70.
Page 64:   1. Adam in the Qur'an (2:34; 7:11; 17:61) represents mankind as God's deputy among creation.
Page 65:   1. Arabic: *ana 'l-Haqq* ("I am the Truth"), the ecstatic saying of Hallaj, regarding whom see the Glossary.
            2. *mansur*, which is also the name of the tenth-century Sufi, Mansur al-Hallaj, who is famous for saying "I am the Truth" (see further "Hallaj" in the Glossary).
Page 66:   1. The perfect Sufi master is conventionally described by Sufis as the inner reality of the Kaaba in Mecca, towards which the Islamic prayer niches face.
            2. See "I" and "we" in the Glossary.
            3. Two scales and two modes in Persian music, which here refer to different spiritual states. 'Hijaz' is also the name of the region in western Arabia where the Kaaba is located.
Page 67   1. "The burnt up ones" represents the Sufis, while "flames and smoke" refers to cooking at the stove.
            2. "The world-revealing cup of Jamshid" is often used to refer to the heart of the perfected Sufi, although it originates from the story about a cup belonging to the Persian king Jamshid, in which he could see all that is happening in the world.
            3. See "I" and "we" in the Glossary.
Page 68:   1. See "I" and "we" in the Glossary.
            2. *jan*, which also means "soul."
            3. The numerical value of the Persian word for "barley" converts it to the Persian word for "nothing."
Page 71:   1. See "Mahmud and Ayaz" in the Glossary.
Page 73:   1. See "I" and "you" in the Glossary.
Page 74:   1. The letter *alef* in the Persian alphabet is a vertical line.
            2. The letter *nun* in the Persian alphabet takes the form of *u* in English and is written below most other letters.
Page 78:   1. *'ahd*, which also means "era."
            2. *rah-e mokhalef*, translated here as "melody," is a scale in Persian classical music.

NOTES

Page 79:
1. See "I" and "we" in the Glossary.
2. Literally, the water of Zamzam, which refers to a well in Mecca that is believed to have been produced at God's command to provide water for Abraham's son Ishmael and his mother Hagar.

Page 83:
1. See "I" and "we" in the Glossary.

Page 86:
1. Literally, *Takbir*, which is the statement *Allahu Akbar*, meaning "God is Great," and is the opening part of the Muslim call to prayer.
2. See "Mahmud and Ayaz" in the Glossary.

Page 87:
1. Literally, "lazy," and meaning here "undisciplined in spiritual practice."

Page 88:
1. See "I" and "we" in the Glossary.

Page 89:
1. See "I" and "we" in the Glossary.

Page 90:
1. Expounders of religious law.

Page 91:
1. See "I" and "you" in the Glossary.

Page 93:
1. See "I" and "you" in the Glossary.

Page 94:
1. See "I" and "you" in the Glossary.

Page 95:
1. See "I" and "you" in the Glossary.

Page 98:
1. Meaning, wine that brings about the lover's annihilation in God, like the wine that caused Mansur Hallaj to exclaim: "I am the Truth" (see further "Hallaj" in the Glossary).
2. In medieval Persian literature, the beloved is often identified as a Turk and described with appropriate characteristics.
3. See "I" and "we" in the Glossary.
4. A reference to the execution by hanging of Hallaj, regarding whom see the Glossary.

Page 102:
1. See "I" and "we" in the Glossary.
2. Affirmation and negation here refer to *La elaha ella'Llah* ("There is no god but God"), where *la* means "no" (negation), and *ella* means "except" (affirmation). See also the Glossary.

Page 103:
1. Arabic: *aya*, which also means "verse" in the context of the Qur'an, which in the Islamic tradition is considered as God speaking through the Prophet Muhammad.

Page 104:
1. See "I" and "we" in the Glossary.

Page 105:
1. *Nur bebakhshidi*, a play on the poet's name that here means "You pardoned Nurbakhsh," but could also mean "You bestowed light."
2. Literally, "You were his customer."

Page 110:
1. This alludes to the reviving breath of Jesus. See further J. Nurbakhsh, *Jesus in the Eyes of the Sufis*, 2nd Edition, London/New York, 2012, pp. 49-52, 164, 169.
2. Literally, "My heart is attached (is a hostage) to your crucifix-like curls."

Page 112:
1. See "I" and "you" in the Glossary.

Page 114:
1. See "I" and "you" in the Glossary.

Page 115:
1. See "I" and "we" in the Glossary.

Page 116:
1. See "I" and "we" in the Glossary.

Page 120:
1. The image here is of a polo bat striking the helpless polo ball.
2. *sheshdar*: a position in backgammon where one player is prevented from playing because the other player has occupied six contiguous spaces so that no throw of the dice will allow the first player's piece to move.
3. Literally, "Who has been checkmated by your rook," where the Persian word for "rook" also means "face" or "cheek."

Page 122:
1. *mehr*, which also means "love."

Page 123:
1. See "I" and "we" in the Glossary.
2. See "we" and "you" in the Glossary.
3. This line may also be translated as "By God [i.e., I swear] I see God!"

Page 126:
1. See "we" and "you" in the Glossary.

NOTES

Page 127: 1. See "I" and "we" in the Glossary.
Page 128: 1. See "I" and "we" in the Glossary.
Page 131: 1. See "I" and "we" in the Glossary.
2. These lines play with the Persian words *peyman* (covenant) and *peymaneh* (measuring cup). Covenant may refer to the vows that the disciple makes during initiation into Sufism and also to the *peyman-e-alast* (Qur'an 7:172), as to which see "Covenant" in the Glossary.
Page 132: 1. *rokh*, which means both rook and face or cheek.
Page 133: 1. In Middle Eastern folklore, buried treasure is often found in ruins, protected by magical spells. Here the "treasure" is love and the "ruins" the lover's heart.
Page 135: 1. i.e., the heart's desire.
2. See note 1 above.
Page 136: 1. "no god" and "but God" are from the Arabic statement *La elaha ella'Llah* ("There is no god but God"). See also the Glossary.
Page 138: 1. A reference to the pre-eternal covenant of *Alast* (see Covenant in the Glossary).
Page 139: 1. *nur nabakhshi*, which can also mean, "If you don't forgive Nurbakhsh."
Page 144: 1. See "I" and "we" in the Glossary.
Page 145: 1. See "I" and "we" in the Glossary.
Page 147: 1. See "I" and "we" in the Glossary.
Page 148: 1. See "I" and "you" in the Glossary.
2. See "we" and "you" in the Glossary.
3. *Shur* and *nava* (pronounced *navaa*) are modal systems of classical Persian music.
Page 150: 1. See "I" and "we" in the Glossary.
2. See "Mahmud and Ayaz" in the Glossary.
Page 151: 1. *Hayy-o hu* represents passionate shouts but also alludes to the vocal *zekr* performed by Sufis, which often involves chanting the names of God *Hayy* (the Ever-Living) and *Hu* (the Indefinable Essence of God).
Page 152: 1. See "we" and "you" in the Glossary.
Page 154: 1. See "I" and "we" in the Glossary.
Page 155: 1. See "we" and "you" in the Glossary.
2. See "I" and "we" in the Glossary.
Page 156: 1. See "Mahmud and Ayaz" in the Glossary.
Page 159: 1. See "I" and "we" in the Glossary.
Page 160: 1. See "I" and "you" in the Glossary.
Page 161: 1. Literally, "I became without head and foot."
Page 163: 1. See "you" and "we" in the Glossary.
2. See "I" and "you" in the Glossary.
Page 164: 1. "He is *Hu*" is a play on words since "*Hu*" means the pronoun "he" as well as God's essence (see *Hu* in the Glossary).
Page 165: 1. See "I" and "we" in the Glossary.
Page 168: 1. See "I" and "you" in the Glossary.
Page 169: 1. See "I" and "we" in the Glossary.
Page 170: 1. See "I" and "you" in the Glossary.
Page 174: 1. See "we" and "you" in the Glossary.
2. *Shah-i ke darad Ne'mat Allahi* ("the King who has God's bounty") is an allusion to Shah Ne'matollah, the founder of the Nimatullahi Sufi Order.
Page 177: 1. See "I" and "we" in the Glossary.
Page 179: 1. See "I" and "we" in the Glossary.
Page 180: 1. *La elaha ella'Llah* is Arabic for "There is no god but God," which is often understood by Sufis to mean that nothing exists but God. See also the Glossary.

NOTES

Page 182:   1. See "we" and "you" in the Glossary.
            2. See "I" and "we" in the Glossary.
Page 183:   1. See "I" and "you" in the Glossary.
Page 184:   1. See "Farhad and Shirin" in the Glossary.
Page 187:   1. See "I" and "you" in the Glossary.
Page 189:   1. See "I" and "we" in the Glossary.
Page 192:   1. See "I" and "we" in the Glossary.
Page 193:   1. See "I" and "we" in the Glossary.
Page 198:   1. See "we" and "you" in the Glossary.
Page 202:   1. The word translated here as "sweet" is *shirin*, which is also the name of Shirin, the beloved of Farhad in a well-known Persian love poem. The word translated here as "lover" is Farhad in the original. See "Farhad and Shirin" in the Glossary.
Page 206:   1. The word translated here as "water" is the Arabic word *ma*, which means "we" in Persian.
Page 207:   1. See "I" and "we" in the Glossary.
Page 209:   1. In this line, the word *rokh*, translated as "face," can also mean a rook in chess, and the word *mat*, translated as "awestruck," can also mean "checkmated."
            2. *ahadiyyat*: Divine Oneness at the level where no differentiations whatsoever exist. See further J. Nurbakhsh, *Sufi Symbolism*, Vol. XIV, pp. 141-3.
            3. *wahediyyat*: Divine Oneness at the level where the archetypes are manifest within Oneness. See further J. Nurbakhsh, *Sufi Symbolism*, Vol. XIV, pp. 148-50.
Page 210:   1. *Noruz*: the festival of the Persian new year.
Page 212:   1. Literally, "water and clay," i.e. the human body.
Page 213:   2. See "I" and "you" in the Glossary.
Page 214:   1. *morgh-e haqq*, which is the Persian name for the screech owl, whose cry sounds like a Sufi chanting "*Hu*," and also means "the bird of God/the Truth."
            2. See "I" and "we" in the Glossary.
Page 215:   3. Majnun and Farhad are both lovers in two different love stories. From love, Majnun becomes frail and helpless while Farhad becomes powerful and tireless. See "Majnun" and "Farhad" in the Glossary.
Page 224:   1. See "I" and "you" in the Glossary.
            2. "There is no God" and "only God" are quoted from the Arabic statement *La elaha ella'Llah* ("There is no deity but God"). See also the Glossary.
Page 227:   1. Literally, "…here is the perfect playing field and ball."
Page 229:   1. See "I" and "you" in the Glossary.
            2. See "we" and "you" in the Glossary.
Page 231:   1. *morad*, which means both "object of desire" and "master."
            2. *ravan*, which means both "psyche" and "motion."
            3. See "we" and "you" in the Glossary.
Page 233:   1. See "I" and "you" in the Glossary.
Page 234:   1. See "I" and "we" in the Glossary.
Page 235:   1. See "I" and "we" in the Glossary.
Page 240:   1. See "I" and "we" in Glossary.
Page 244:   2. Shams of Tabriz was the master of the famous Sufi poet Jelal al-Din Rumi (d.1273).
Page 251:   1. Begging bowls and axes were among the common objects carried by wandering dervishes and are still used today as symbols of the Nimatullahi Sufi Order.
Page 252:   2. See "I" and "we" in the Glossary.
            3. See "we" and "you" in the Glossary.
Page 254:   1. In Persian literature, long quests are often described as traversing seven valleys. The holes of the Persian reed flute divide the instrument into seven segments, distinct from reed flutes in other regions (e.g. the Turkish reed flute of nine segments).

NOTES

Page 256: 2. See "we" and "you" in the Glossary.
Page 263: 1. See "I" and "we" in the Glossary.
Page 265: 2. The Simorgh is a phoenix-like mythical bird, famous in English as the goal of the mystical path in Attar's poem, *The Conference of the Birds*.
3. In Persian cosmology, Mount Qaf refers to a range of mountains that surrounds the world and marks the border with the spiritual realm.
4. Rakhsh is the name of the extraordinarily fast and strong horse of Rostam, the hero of the Persian epic, *The Book of Kings*.
Page 266: 1. This verse integrates within the Persian poetry Arabic citations from the Qur'an that describe God's creation of the world and the breathing of life into creatures.
Page 274: 1. See "I" and "we" in the Glossary.
Page 277: 2. See "Bayazid" in the Glossary.
3. Shemr was the commander of the caliph Yazid (see the Glossary), who on the latter's instruction massacred Husayn ebn Ali and his supporters in Kerbala, Iraq, in 680.
Page 280: 1. See "I" and "we" in the Glossary.
Page 281: 2. See "Bayazid" in the Glossary.
Page 285: 1. See "Bayazid" in the Glossary.
2. See "Yazid" in the Glossary.
Page 295: 1. The *saqinameh* (Ode to the Cupbearer) is a popular genre of Persian poetry. It is conventional for a Persian poet's collection, or *Divan*, to contain a few examples of this genre, such as this and the following two poems. They are written in rhyming couplets and address the cupbearer with an appeal for wine.
Page 296: 1. See note 1 above.
Page 298: 1. See note 1 above.
2. See "I" and "we" in the Glossary.
Page 299: 3. This line alludes to the Sufi division of God into an unknowable Essence and a definable set of attributes.
Page 305: 1. The complete title of this poem is "Composed in 1949 by Order of Munis Ali Shah in Response to One of the Brothers on the Spiritual Path." Munis Ali Shah was the master of the Nimatullahi Order immediately prior to Dr. Nurbakhsh, who was 23 years old at the time this poem was written.
Page 306: 2. The image of "the novice Magian" represents the divinely attracted mystic (see further *mogh-bachah* in J. Nurbakhsh, *Sufi Symbolism*, Vol. III, p. 216).
Page 308: 1. A reference to the divine name (*zekr*) placed upon the heart of the disciple by the master during initiation in some Sufi orders.
2. See "I" and "we" in the Glossary.
Page 313: 1. See "I" and "you" in the Glossary.
Page 321: 1. See "I" and "you" in the Glossary.
Page 322: 2. See "I" and "we" in the Glossary.
3. An allusion to the Islamic image of the human body being made of water and clay.
Page 324: 4. See "I" and "you" in the Glossary.
5. See "I" and "we" in the Glossary.
Page 326: 6. *ma'im hame*, which can also mean, "it is all me."
7. See "I" and "we" in the Glossary.
Page 332: 1. For the symbolic use of "beauty mark" or "mole" in Sufi poetry, see J. Nurbakhsh, *Sufi Symbolism*, Vol. I, pp. 44-7.
Page 337: 2. *Qiamat*, which also means "Day of Resurrection," which signals the end of time in Islamic eschatology.
Page 339: 3. See "I" and "we" in the Glossary.

NOTES

Page 346: 4. *sheshdar*: a position in backgammon where one player is prevented from playing because the other player has occupied six contiguous spaces so that no throw of the dice will allow the first player's piece to move.

Page 351: 5. "*La*" refers to the Arabic word for "No," as used in *La elaha ella'Llah* ("There is no god but God"). See also the Glossary.

Page 354: 6. Qur'an 2:115.

Page 359: 7. Contraction (*qabz*) is a mystical state on the Sufi path (see further J. Nurbakhsh, *Sufism*, Vol. II, pp. 27-40).

8. See Covenant in the Glossary.

9. A reference to the *hadith* (prophetic tradition) in which the Prophet Muhammad supplicates, "O God, show me all things as they truly are!"

Page 360: 10. Contraction (*qabz*) and expansion (*bast*) are mystical states on the Sufi path (see further J. Nurbakhsh, *Sufism*, Vol. II, pp. 27-40).

Page 361: 11. Part of a saying of the Prophet Muhammad recorded in the *hadith* literature about his exclusive experiences with God.

Page 362: 12. See "I" and "we" in the Glossary.

Page 363: 13. See "Covenant" in the Glossary.

14. See "Mahmud and Ayaz" in the Glossary.

15. God is frequently referred to in the Qur'an as the All-Seeing (*al-Basir*).

Page 364: 16. The original is a Persian translation of Qur'an 17:81.

Page 367: 17. For the symbolic uses of parts of the face of the Beloved in Sufi poetry, see J. Nurbakhsh, *Sufi Symbolism*, Vol. I.

Page 368: 18. Literally, Rafraq, one of the creatures upon which the Prophet Muhammad made his Night Journey to God.

Page 369: 19. In the Persian alphabet, one letter is often distinguished from another by the placement of one or more dots above it.

Page 370: 20. See Covenant in the Glossary.

Page 374: 21. i.e., how God is contained in the heart.

Page 375: 22. This is a shortened form of an Arabic formula commonly repeated by Muslims: "No force or power exists but through God, the All-High, the Tremendous."

Page 376: 23. See "we" and "you" in the Glossary.

Page 383: 24. See "we" and "you" in the Glossary.

ACKNOWLEDGMENTS

Thanks to Mahan Azadpour, David Cagan, Alisa Cherkasova, Alexa Davidson, Irina Dorochenko, Rita Fabrizio, Doug Gilbert, Mary Gossy, Lenni Gutierrez, Emmet McDonald, Chara Nelson, Mohammad Nooraee, Safoura Nourbakhsh, Radhika Ochalik, David Paquiot, Samantha Paquiot, Lolo Saney, Fahad Siadat, Patricia Sweeney, Kadar Villanueva, Aisha Weber and Ona Weber.

PHOTO CREDITS

Page 1 - Ocean Wave | Hengki Koentjoro, page 220 - xuanhuongho | IStock.com, page 292 - Jacob H | IStock.com, page 302 - Grecu Mihail Alin | Dreamstime.com, page 310 - Ivan Olelenko, page 318 - Lake Lite | Lucy Loomis, page 328 - Ivan Olelenko.